FACTORIES AND FAMILIES

A Study of a Growth Pole in South India

FACTORIES AND FAMILIES

A Study of a Growth Pole in South India

Edited by
J. J. F. Heins
E. N. Meijer
K. W. Kuipers

MANOHAR
1992

ISBN 81-7304-003-6

First Published 1992

Published by
Ajay Kumar Jain
Manohar Publishers and Distributors
2/6 Ansari Road, Darya Ganj
New Delhi

Printed at
Rajkamal Electric Press
G.T. Karnal Road
Delhi

CONTENTS

PREFACE

This book presents the findings of research conducted in Hosur, a small town near Bangalore, during the period 1985-1990. The study focused on the impact of growth pole policy implemented by the state government of Tamil Nadu on the development of the backward Dharmapuri district. The development potential of recently created new small-scale activities, and the position and prospects of underprivileged and vulnerable groups in local society are the two central questions for this evaluation of growth pole policy.

The research on which this book is based, formed part of the research programme of the Geography Departments of both Amsterdam universities, and it was carried out in cooperation with the sister faculty at the University of Madras. In the research projects students from different scientific disciplines participated. Their individual research reports form the empirical base of this book.

This research would never have been completed without the help of many people and institutions. We owe a great deal to Mr. N. Ramalingam, former Member-Secretary of the New Town Development Authority of Hosur for his useful information and the interest he took in our work. We also want to express our gratitude to Mr. A. Abdus Salam, our main local field assistant who was invaluable to the research. Prof. Dr. G.A. de Bruijne was kind enough to give comments on an earlier draft. However, the usual disclaimer applies for the remaining mistakes.

Finally, we are deeply indebted to the many informants in Hosur, who frankly and patiently contributed to this research, ant who are entitled to enjoy a larger share of its fruits than they probably will.

The editors

1. HOSUR, THE RAPID GROWTH OF A SMALL TOWN; AN INTRODUCTION

Ko Heins and Evert Meijer

The second part of the eighties in India has been characterized by a strong emphasis on urban modernization and maximum economic growth. This may lead to increasing inequality in income between social groups and regions. In due course the spread of income will automatically reduce disparities. However, followers of Gandhian development views reject the idea of spontaneous processes leading to equality. In their view, development starts at the bottom of society: in the backward districts with the poor villagers.

In this study the continuous struggle between both views of development will be analyzed by investigating the case of a growth pole in a backward area. In the South Indian context, the poor agricultural district of Dharmapuri in Tamil Nadu forms a striking contrast with the rapidly developing modern city of Bangalore. The regional development policy of the government of Tamil Nadu aims at diminishing the spatial inequalities by means of a growth pole policy. The establishment of new industrial estates in Hosur is based on the modernization paradigm, with a maximum increase of production as the main goal. However the question arises whether this policy leads to the creation of employment and welfare for the original population of the Dharmapuri district.
Various aspects of the development of Hosur will be dealt with in subsequent chapters. In this introductory chapter we begin with a brief discussion of regional development strategies for small towns in India. After a description of the study area, the main themes concerning the effects of growth pole policy are presented.

1.1 Small town development in India

The role of small towns in socio-economic development has generated a substantial amount of literature, most of it in favor of the encouragement of small town development (Hardoy and Satterthwaite 1986). Despite the paradigm shift that characterizes certain theories of development as they have been applied to the Third World, there has not been much change in the assertion that small towns play a beneficial role in spreading development to the underdeveloped hinterlands they service. Urban areas are seen as progressive and modernizing in

contr·st to the stagnant and backward rural areas. They are the disseminating s for the spread of development. The growth of small urban centers is also (lered as an attractive policy designed to reverse polarized growth focused o large urban centers.
S critics, however, argue that there is little evidence that induced growth ce ; have generated significant spread effects in their economically lagging hinterlands (Friedmann 1979). The diffusion of innovation required for trickle-down effects assumes a homogeneous transport and/or communication system and ignores the influence of cultural practices. Wong and Saigol (1984) compared the economic impacts of six growth centers on their surrounding rural areas in Asia. They found more unfavorable than favorable impacts of growth centers on their surrounding rural areas.

In the Fifth Plan (1974-1979), the government of India formulated among other objectives, the development of smaller urban centers and the strengthening of local authorities in implementing urban development schemes. But the urban development programs were regarded as social welfare schemes, outside the mainstream of national development. In addition, the physical plans lacked economic, social and political content; the preparation of masterplans for small and intermediate urban centers appeared at random and were devoid of both economic analysis and development orientation. Mohan (1983) reported on the result of offering incentives to industries to establish in 'backward areas'. Districts designated in this way cover around 60 per cent of India's entire population and 70 per cent of its total area. Industry has not invested in some of the least backward areas. Almost 90 per cent of the concessional investment funds went to just 22 districts and most of these were near metropolitan areas. Furthermore, at least three of the metropolitan cities (New Delhi, Bangalore and Hyderabad) had 'backward areas' in their backyards (i.e. in adjacent districts). Not surprisingly, private industry has been quite happy to take advantage of the incentives given for establishing in these areas, but this hardly provides much stimulus to poorer areas.

In the seventies, the state government started a policy in Tamil Nadu that aimed at diminishing the spatial inequalities by means of a two-pronged approach (De Bruijne a.o. 1983):
- defensive planning, i.e. regulation and control of the growth of Madras; and
- offensive planning, i.e. stimulation of the development of a restricted number of (regional) growth poles (second and third order towns).

With this policy the government has chosen to generate selective growth from a restricted number of nuclei and not to spread growth more evenly. Regional development was to be achieved by economic growth of functional networks.
The State Industries Promotion Corporation of Tamil Nadu Ltd. (SIPCOT) has been the agency for implementing both the central and the state incentives for industrial development in backward areas. This institute acts as an agent of the central government for disbursing the 15 per cent central investment subsidy and

it also acts as the agent for state government in administering the interest free sales tax loans schemes. For small-scale units, another agency undertakes similar promotional activities: the Small Industries Development Corporation (SIDCO) of Tamil Nadu.
Hosur is an example of successful implementation by SIPCOT of the above policies. Infrastructural facilities like developed land, water, electricity, roads etc. have been provided in this small town and taluk headquarters. Within a period of 10 years more than 100 companies have located here.
These firms were attracted by financial incentives (loans, subsidies, exemption of import duty) that can account for between 32% (small units) and 40% (for large firms) of the investment costs. The total investment in the SIPCOT estate is estimated on Rs 100 - 150 crore (1 crore Rs ≈ US$ 1 million) (Bharathan 1981; SIPCOT[1]). Among major companies are Ashok Leyland (transport equipment, investment Rs 37 crore), Asia Tobacco (cigarettes, Rs 10 crore) and Lakshmi (textile, Rs 9 crore). There are also a number of companies that settled outside the SIPCOT estate. For instance a large establishment of the TVS-group (i.a. transport equipment) is located at 8 km from Hosur. Total employment on the SIPCOT estate is around 10,000, and the TVS-group employs around 3000.

1.2 Hosur, a town in the Dharmapuri district

One of the most backward areas of Tamil Nadu is the Dharmapuri district. In 1981, only 9.4% of the population was urban and the Dharmapuri district had the lowest urban to total population ratio in Tamil Nadu. It had a population of almost 2 million living on a total area of 9622 km^2, and the population density of 208 per square km in the Dharmapuri district was the lowest density in Tamil Nadu (average 372). The literacy rate here was lowest in Tamil Nadu with only 29% of the people being able to read and write 'with understanding' (average 47%). The large majority of the workers were cultivators or agricultural laborers (83%) (Census 1981). Dharmapuri is a dry area with scanty rainfall, rightly described as a backward area.

Hosur[2] is located on the main road (National Highway No. 7) that connects Bangalore and Madras. It is situated quite near to the border with Karnataka at a distance of only 45 km from Bangalore, which is the fifth city of India with more than 4 million inhabitants (see map 1).

[1] Investment estimation is based on a list of allotees in Sipcot Industrial Complex Hosur (April 1985) with the size of the area allotted and for most firms the initial investments.

[2] "The name Hosur is the Kanarees equivalent for 'New Town'. Hosur is said to have been founded by Gutalu Gurappa Nayanivaru, the first of the Bagalur Poligars, who built a fort, a palace and temples." (Salem Gazeteer 1918: 137).

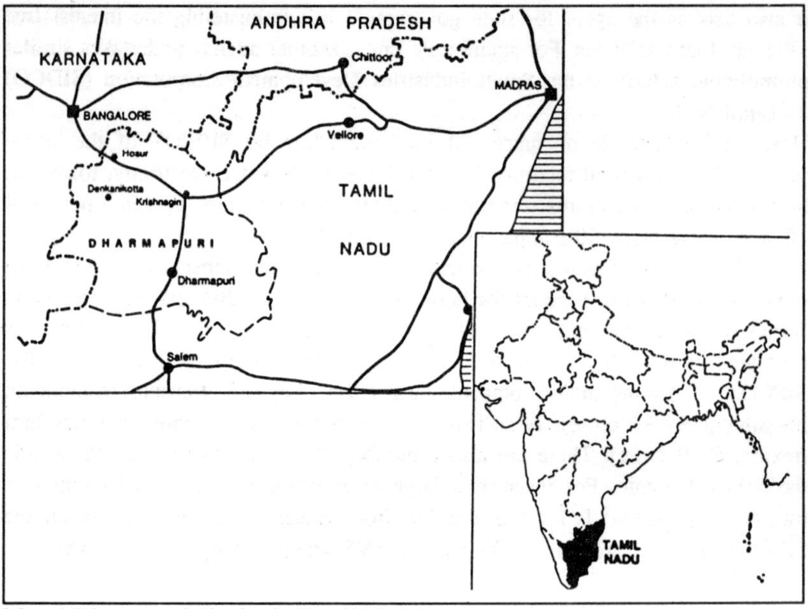

Map 1 Dharmapuri district in Tamil Nadu

At the end of the eighteenth century, Hosur came under British authority after the Mysore wars with the Muslim leader, Tippu Sultan. There were a number of serious famines in the nineteenth century. "There was famine in the district during the years 1833 and 1876 till 1878 and severe scarcity in 1866 and 1891 till 1892". (Statistical Atlas Salem District 1908: 13). According to the Salem Gazeteer (1918), the houses were of poor quality and the town was feverish and pest-epidemics ravaged the place every year. The population of Hosur decreased in 1876-1878 with 18.6%. In 1901 the population of Hosur was still 4.2% under the level of 1871.

The population development of Hosur between 1891 and 1985 is described in table 1.1.

Table 1.1 Population change in Hosur 1891-1985

Year	Population	Average annual % increase
1891	5,756	
1901	6,695	1.63
1911	5,913	-1.17
1921	5,513	-0.68
1931	6,071	1.01
1941	6,457	0.64
1951	8,712	3.50
1961	11,683	3.40
1971	16,591	4.20
1981	27,129	6.35
1985	35,000 (estimate)	6.45

Source: Census of India 1971: District Census Handbook Dharmapuri district: 194-195
own survey 1985.

The seize of the population was during the first half of the century in general stable and the growth rate low. The fast increase of Hosur in the seventies (it exceeded the decennial growth of the urban population of Tamil Nadu 1971-1981 at 28.0%), has continued during the first part of the eighties. Only one comparable town in Tamil Nadu also had an average annual percentage increase of more than 5% (being Ramaswaran in the Ramanathapuran district).

The rise in population has led to the development of a number of new residential areas. In map 2, the built-up area of the town has been divided into nine parts grouped as follows:
- four central areas divided by main streets (predominantly the old parts of the town);
- a southern part with middle class residential developments;
- a big HUDCO housing scheme in the north;
- some other, at different places located, middle class housing schemes; and
- two Economically Weakest Section (EWS)-areas.

In table 1.2 the number of counted households, the average household size and the estimated population of each of the parts are presented.

Table 1.2 The population of Hosur, 1985[3]

	Number of households	Average household size	Total population
1. Bagalore Housing Scheme	850	3.8	3230
2. Other schemes	750	3.8	2850
3. Central North East	950	5.3	5035
4. Central North West	450	6.0	2700
5. Central South East	675	5.6	3780
6. Central South West	1150	4.2	4830
7. South	850	4.2	3570
8. Therpetai (EWS)	1000	5.3	5300
9. Ram Nagar (EWS)	800	3.5	2800
Total Hosur	7475	4.6	34095

Source: own survey 1985.

The differences between the average household size in the nine parts can partly be explained by the general socio-economic status of the households. Mainly middle and upper class people, whose households are relatively small, live in the housing schemes. Only the extremely small average household size in Ram Nagar, an EWS-area, contradicts the correlation between socio-economic position and household size. The average number of persons per household (4.6) has slightly diminished since the 1981 Census. The population of 27,129 was then divided among 5536 households, with an average household size of 4.9. At that time the average urban household size in the Dharmapuri District was 5.7 as opposed to 5.1 in whole urban Tamil Nadu.

[3] Because there are several pockets of houses in the outskirts of the built-up area, a reasonable estimate of the population of Hosur in mid-1985 is 35,000 persons.

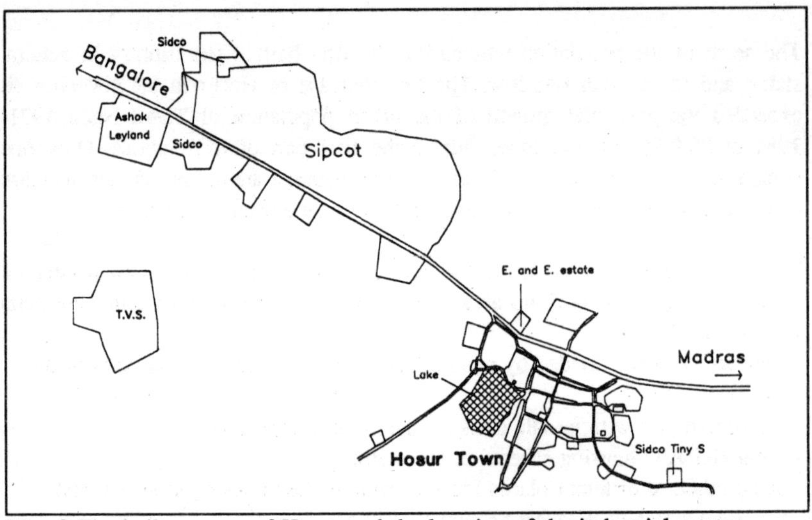

Map 2 The built-up area of Hosur and the location of the industrial estates

1.3 Main themes of the effects of growth pole policy

The following chapters will discuss some of the effects of the growth pole policy on the development of Hosur and in its hinterlands. Chapter 2 will give a treatment of the industrial policy of Hosur. It particularly deals with the small-scale industrial sector and its linkages with the larger-scale sector. The growth in the number of large and medium-scale industries in the area has resulted in extensive growth in the small-scale sector, in the way the 'trickle-down effect' would predict. A closer look at the inter-firm relations, however, reveals that a trickle-down as such is not enough to ensure a sustained growth in the small-scale sector and job security for those working in this sector. The bargaining position of the employees in the small-scale sector may be in general very weak and consequently their vulnerability is high. The bargaining strength of small-scale units is also weak. Mainly, it is the technician-entrepreneur that faces difficulties in establishing the necessary contracts with the purchasing officers of larger-scale units. Small-scale enterprises that produce finished products operate different from units in the input sector. Ancillarization may solve the problems of irregularities in orders and lack of working capital.

The new industries have created a demand for mainly skilled laborers, who were not available in Hosur. Chapter 3 shows that the majority of the migrants are recruited from the big cities in Tamil Nadu. Most of the migrants are young men, often bachelors, whose existence throws the age structure of Hosur out of balance. Indirect effects of the growth of Hosur on migration have been minor;

migration from the rural hinterland has not increased substantially. Some of the short-distance migrants found a job in the SIPCOT industries, though only at the lower paid levels. The demographic future of Hosur is, in particular, connected with the spatial behavior of the bachelors, but commuting may also play a role. Many people travel daily from the surrounding areas and Bangalore to the industrial estates. Also Hosur itself attracts commuters from the rural areas. Their characteristics and the relations between commuting and migration are more specific analyzed in chapter 4. Commuting can have effects on both the individuals and the households they belong to. The increase of employment opportunities, the improved change to acquire training in different kind of jobs and the preservation of social ties can be considered as positive effects on the individual. Stimulating effects at the household level are the increase of the total household budget, the spreading of risks, the contacts made with new, differently structured labor markets, and possibly an opportunity for saving. Important is also to find out how migrants themselves adapt with respect to housing and work. Relatives and friends may play a dominant role with the obtainment of a house. In particular, circular migrants will live with relatives or rent a room. A permanent migrant is more likely to prefer a house of his own. Chapter 4 also deals with the way migrants get information about the new place of residence and the employment opportunities available. Further attention will be paid to a housing area of poor in-migrants in Hosur, Ram Nagar.

The growth of industries has led to a spectacular increase in different kinds of paid and unpaid labor. Chapter 5 will examine the labor markets for women. There are three different labor markets: the formal (officially organized labor in, for example, large-scale capitalistic enterprises), the informal (unofficially organized labor in small-scale units) and the shadow labor market where no money is transferred for production. Because of sexe-segregation in these labor markets the place of women's work is always in the bottom segment. This implies for each segment the lowest paid work with the lowest status. The division of unpaid work between the sexes is pretty fixed; as long as women are part of the household, men will not do unpaid work in the household.
Unskilled laborers in factories or in workshops and the building industry are discussed in chapter 6. Unskilled labor has been defined as labor for which no special training, education or knowledge is required for the worker and which can be done by any one at any time. The workers who do this type of work certainly do not correspond with unskilled workers! In this chapter case-studies have been made of labor conditions of workers who perform unskilled labor, and the possibilities for improving these conditions. The construction industry and the building material market are also analyzed in this chapter.
The growth pole policy in Hosur has given rise to a lot of new developments and the expansion of existing activities. But the provision of housing and facilities like water-supply, health care and education has not kept pace with the development of employment and population growth. In the four dry months, from February till June, the wells, pumps and taps provide no more than 25% of the demand for water. In the near future, the building of the new Kavaranapalli

dam outside Hosur-town will bring a solution for the irrigation problems in agriculture and the water shortages of the industrial area. In the short term, it will give no relief to the population of Hosur itself. Chapter 7 deals with these water problems.

In particular poor people have a limited access to housing and work. They usually find places in the outskirts of the town and on the marginal lands. The poorest find employment in vulnerable economic activities like ragpicking and as such play a role in the waste recycling industry of the town. A case-study has been made of the ragpickers group of Hosur and is presented in chapter 8.

In the last chapter some general conclusions are drawn concerning the effects of the spatial policy pursued by the Tamil Nadu government, in particular for the poorest section of the population of Hosur.

2. Industrial Policy and the Role of Small-Scale Industries

Peter Knorringa

This chapter deals with the industrial structure and especially the role of small-scale enterprises within that structure. In Hosur the metal-based sectors, who have strong interlinkages between different production units, are dominant. Most of the medium-scale general engineering units are forging and casting units, who obtain the bulk of their orders from other factories in the area. Moreover, some of the large industrial houses in India have set up plants in the Hosur area. Several of them are connected to foreign multinational firms. A noteworthy example is TVS, which has a large complex located near Hosur. TVS, a joint venture with the multinational Suzuki, occupies a special place in the industrial structure of Hosur, because of its typical Japanese management style. Through Suzuki not only technology is imported but also a system of norms and values is coming across. The, mainly skilled, laborers that work on the TVS complex have company clothing, good secondary labor conditions when compared with the average large-scale unit in Hosur, and they undertake several joint social activities.

Multi-plant industrial firms often have more than one unit located in Hosur, units that depend on other plants from the same industrial house for orders. A fine tuned division of tasks between different types of production units has evolved in these sectors, resulting in a complex network of interlinkages. The metal-based small-scale units are almost never really part of one of the dominant industrial houses. Their scale of operation, level of specialization and their large numbers make that they are incorporated in the industrial structure on a more loose basis, through the least advantageous type of subcontracting: job-work.
The general production structure in Hosur is overwhelmingly oriented towards the national and international markets. That part of the small-scale sector that is not incorporated through subcontracting mostly operates in the niches of the market left by the large-scale sector: the local market and to a lesser extent the regional market. The larger-scale units on the SIPCOT estate are, on the one hand, linked to head offices in Bangalore and Madras and, on the other hand, for as far as subcontracting relations are present, to the local economy through linkages with the small-scale sector in Hosur. This town is for the main group of large-scale enterprises only a center of production. There are hardly backward linkages concerning raw materials with the rural hinterland.

The growth pole policy consists of two types of programmes (Bharatan 1981). These are:

A. Financial incentives:

1. The 'central scheme of investment subsidy';
2. The 'interest free sales tax loan scheme', which is a state government scheme; and
3. Provision of term loans at concessional rates by the term lending institutions.

B. Physical infrastructure:

4. Provision of industrial infrastructure in the form of developed plots, assured industrial water, etc. in the form of industrial estates; and
5. Provision of social requirements such as housing, drinking water, medical facilities and education.

Three estates have been set up at Hosur: the SIPCOT and SIDCO area and the Electrical and Electronics Estate. The majority of the factories are located on one of the estates, but several are located away from them. All the units in the Electrical and Electronics Estate are small-scale units.

It is striking that only four companies on the SIPCOT and SIDCO industrial area employ nearly half of the industrial labor (table 2.1). In particular the small companies of the SIDCO estate have in average no more than ten workers.

Table 2.1 Number of companies on SIPCOT and SIDCO[1] industrial area by number of employees, 1986

Number of employees	companies	total number of employees
3 - 10	90	900
10 - 30	65	1,300
30 - 100	15	900
100 - 200	14	1,900
200 - 400	5	1,200
400 - 1900	4	4,400
Total	193	10,600

Source: SIPCOT information and own survey 1986.

Together with the growth in the large- and medium-scale sector there has also been substantial growth in the small-scale sector[2]. The growth manifests itself in both the industrial and service sectors. The data collection was restricted to small-scale units in the manufacturing sector with a fixed investment of less than Rs 20 lakh[3] that can also not be seen as household industries[4]. The small-scale

[1] This includes only the SIDCO industrial estates located close to the SIPCOT area.

[2] Data collection in September - December 1986.

[3] According to the official definition, see SIPCOT (1984), p. 4.

sector in Hosur consists mainly of general engineering units (metal-based), units operating in the wood sector and paper-based sectors such as printing[5]. The remaining group of small-scale units is far from homogeneous as will be shown below.

2.1 Small-scale industries in Hosur

In the early seventies Hosur was a 'sleeping' town with fewer than 10 metal-based small-scale units working for local needs[6]. In 1986 there were more than hundred small-scale enterprises in the manufacturing sector in Hosur-town and another hundred on the small-scale sector industrial estates. In Hosur-town, 71% of the units now in operation have started their production after 1982 (see table 2.2). In 1985 and 1986 there has been a growth of 91% in the number of operating units. On the small-scale industrial estates the large influx started in 1979, when the first two estates were officially opened. Here, 56% of the units have started since 1983. Although one-fourth of the ready-built sheds are not used at present, growth seems to be faltering. Still, in the last two years there has been a growth of 30% in the number of units. A large growth in itself, but only one-third of the explosive growth of small-scale enterprises in town. In interpreting these growth data, it is important to realize that only the units in operation in 1986 could be counted. Undoubtedly, there will be a number of units that does not longer exist, but these units were in operation in the late seventies and early eighties.

Table 2.2 Starting year of units in operation end 1986

	Town		Ind.Estates		Total	
	abs.	cum.%	abs.	cum.%	abs.	cum.%
up to '76	9	9%	1	1%	10	5%
'77 - '80	10	18%	26	27%	36	23%
'81 - '82	11	29%	17	44%	28	37%
'83 - '84	24	52%	33	77%	57	65%
'85 - '86	49	100%	23	100%	72	100%
Total	103		100		203	

Source: own survey 1986.

2.1.1 Types of industries

In this section the small-scale units will be subdivided into four main groups. A first rough subdivision within the small-scale sector is the one between workshops and small-scale factories. In general, the units in town can be

[4] See for a definition of household industries Kalpagam (1984), p. 202.

[5] Food-processing was excluded.

[6] This information stems from local, elder, entrepreneurs and other key informants.

classified as workshops, those on the estates as small-scale factories. Data from the survey corroborate a distinction between town and estates. The scale of operations, in terms of employment, turnover and investment, is clearly larger on the small-scale estates as compared with town. Also, the technology used on the small-scale estates is in general somewhat more advanced than in town and the style of entrepreneurship is more formalized on the small-scale estates. There are of course exceptions. But for instance units in town that operate on a larger scale, in terms of employees, in general still bear greater resemblance with other units in town than with units on the estates that have a similar number of employees. Therefore, the distinction between units located in town and those on the estates will be used.

The forward linkages are seen as crucial in the analysis of the position of the small-scale sector in the economic structure. An important factor determining the form of the linkages is the type of product manufactured. A basic difference exists between enterprises producing finished products and those producing inputs for other industries. This is the second subdivision used. Units producing inputs for other industries are in general far more dependent on larger-scale enterprises since they undertake a part of their production process. These intermediate products are not generally marketable, but usually made on specifications by the large-scale unit. Enterprises manufacturing finished products have in principle a wider marketing scope. This distinction often coincides with the two different types of forward linkages: production for the market and subcontracting. Subcontracting is a specific form of inter-firm relations. Because it is usually a relation between firms with a different amount of bargaining power; there is, in the absence of appropriate government measures, scope for dominance. There are a number of different ways to categorize subcontracting relations. The first is from the perspective of the performed activity[7] by the subcontractor:

- product subcontracting. The subcontractor manufactures the entire product and the larger-scale enterprise does the marketing and gives its name to the product.
- activity subcontracting. The subcontractor handles one of the des-integrated parts of the production process as, for instance, in the cotton industry.
- component subcontracting. The subcontractor delivers one or more of the components of a final product produced by the larger-scale enterprise as, for instance, in metal and automobile industries.
- assembly subcontracting. The subcontractor takes care of the labor- and skill-intensive assembly as, for instance, in the electronics industry.
- job-work contracts. The larger-scale enterprise also supplies the raw materials. The subcontractor executes a labor-intensive operation that can range from machining or cutting the materials provided, to drilling or polishing an existing component or product.

[7] Based on Nagaraj (1984), Panini (1978) and Holmström (1984).

- labor-jobs. Labor-jobs are repair and maintenance, of a supporting nature, of machinery in larger-scale enterprises.

Another way to describe subcontracting relations is by way of the organizational perspective. This deals with the degree to which the relation resembles more a market type of transaction or whether the subcontractor functions more or less as a department of production within the larger firm, of which ancillarization is a good example. In general, the more specific know-how a subcontracting unit has, the higher it can be placed among the activity types of subcontracting and the more likely the contractor would like the subcontractor to become really part of the 'family'. This is also because when the subcontractor performs a more essential part of the total production process his bargaining power towards the contractor is larger and a situation of interdependence arises. Ancillarization is in fact a kind of long-term subcontracting agreement whereby the ancillary unit functions almost as a department of production within the larger-scale enterprise. Such contracts include not only market assurances, provided the quality is up to agreed standards, but also technical assistance. The other end of the spectrum is a type of subcontracting that more resembles a market transaction, where there are no assurances concerning follow-up loads, and certainly no technical assistance. This type of subcontracting relations usually occurs in combination with the less specialized jobs.

Subcontracting in the industrial oriented small-scale sector in Hosur is restricted to component subcontracting, job-work and labor-jobs. Small-scale units subject to different forms of subcontracting are all part of the input sector, while all those manufacturing finished products produce for the market. Therefore, the distinction input as opposed to finished is used. The number of units operating in the input sector is roughly twice as large, both in town and on the estates, than the finished-product sector.

2.1.2 Forward linkages with the large-scale sector

The data clearly show the importance of the linkages with the larger-scale sector (see figure 2.1). In town 71% of the small-scale units depend for more than half of their production on the larger-scale enterprises for orders, while 40% works for them exclusively. Here, also, the difference between units producing finished products and those producing intermediary products is clear. Of the input sector in town, 86% works mostly or exclusively for the larger-scale enterprises in the area. For the manufacturers of finished products this is still 47%. On the estates the difference is even clearer. The input producing units produce for their larger counterparts in 79% of the cases. For those producing finished products this is only 22%. Of all small-scale enterprises in the area two-third depends on orders from the larger-scale sector in the area for the main part of their production. This implies that most of the small-scale enterprises have come up because of the presence of the larger-scale sector.

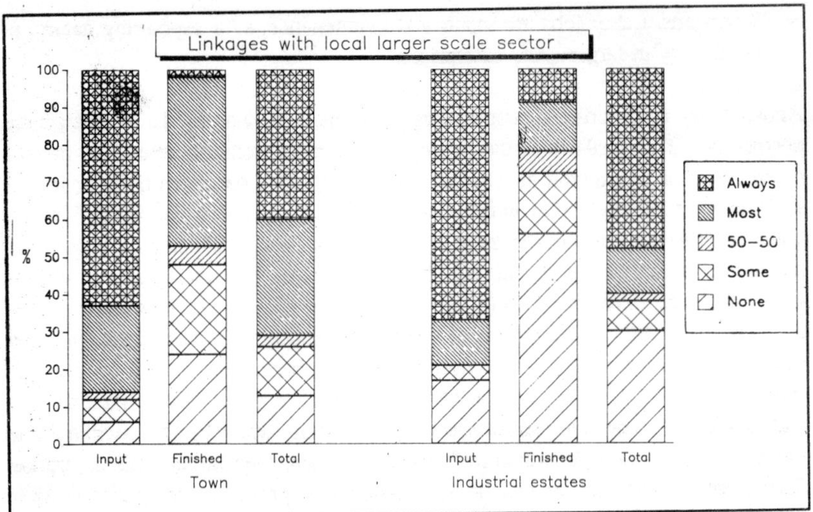

Figure 2.1 Forward linkages with larger-scale sector in the Hosur-area

In figure 2.2 it can be seen that not only the number of small-scale enterprises has increased sharply, but also that their composition by type of activity has changed. The units are classified as having strong linkages or weak linkages with the local larger-scale sector[8]. The number of units with strong linkages has grown much faster than those with weak linkages.

A more detailed study of a, stratified, sample shows that on the estates all units actually work for the large-scale sector. This can be for the locally based (60%) or other large-scale or government enterprises (27%) mainly located in Bangalore. In the finished-product sector, some units sell their products to intermediaries who market these products for them. In this sector some units also sell directly to consumers but never as their main type of clients. In the input sector in town only the repair and maintenance industry, oriented to local parties, do not depend on orders from the large-scale sector. The finished-product sector in town, the most traditional one, is the only sector that works for a substantial part (44%) for local needs. This more detailed picture implies that the percentage of units working for the large-scale sector is even higher when also larger-scale enterprises not locally based are included.

To be able to deal with the implications of the forward linkages of the small-scale units first the situation in the small-scale sector itself must be analyzed. The internal aspects of the small-scale sector are dealt with in the next section, using the two main subdivisions made above: town/estates, input/finished.

---

[8] Based on the division in figure 2.1; 'always', 'mostly' and '50/50' : strong, while 'sometimes' and 'no': weak.

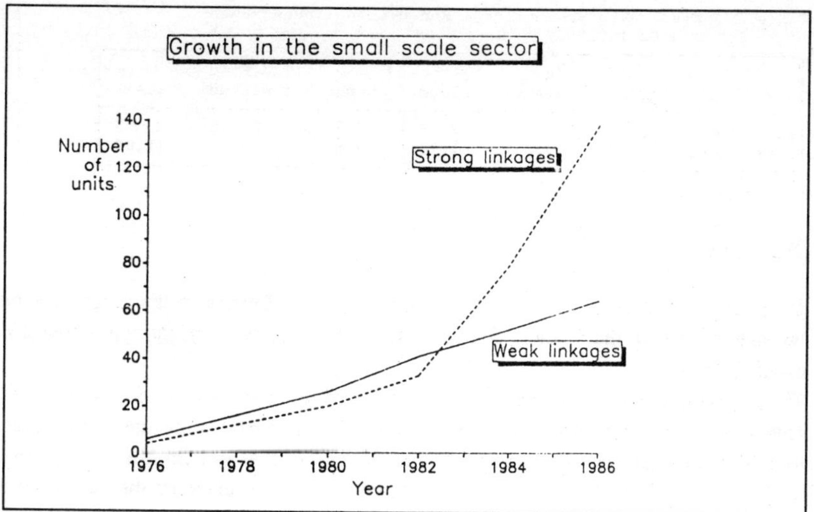

Figure 2.2 Small-scale units classified by type of linkages

2.2 The internal aspects

The first internal aspect is the performance of the small-scale units. The employment generated and the position of the employees is the second aspect. The third internal aspect is the way in which differences in background of the entrepreneur influence performance, and their classification in the labor market.

2.2.1 Performance and results

One of the most striking features of the small-scale sector is the irregularity of working hours, due to a fluctuating quantity of orders. It is common for a unit to work for days on end to complete an order, and to be idle after that until the next 'job' comes through. This also implies that the capacity performance is in general far from optimal. In town 30% of the units work at less than 0.8 of their full-capacity level[9]. On the estates there is even more overcapacity. In two-third of the units, on average less then 0.8 of the capacity is used. Growth in existing units henceforth usually means coming closer to full capacity. Still, in absolute figures the average turnover on the estates exceeds by far the turnover in town. At the same time, the turnover in the input-producing sector is lower than in the finished-product sector (see table 2.3). There is also a wide range within the respective sectors concerning their turnover.
The levels of investment are, on average, almost 9 times larger on the estates than in town. For a more detailed analysis of performance the net profitability can be calculated.

[9] Full-capacity =1

Table 2.3 Average turnover a year and present investment (x Rs 100,000)

	Town			Ind.Est.		
	input	finished	total	input	finished	total
turnover	1.25	3.75	2.15	6.50	26.00	13.00
investment	1.30	1.40	1.30	9.60	13.00	11.00

Source: own survey 1986.

Net profit

In assessing net profit one has to be very cautious. Entrepreneurs might not be willing to reveal the (exact) figures and, moreover, they might not know the exact figures.

Three levels are used to show the different result positions of the small-scale enterprises. The first and lowest level, labelled sick, contains the units with a net loss of more then 5% on average. If their situation does not improve soon, they will have to close down. The second level shows the units in the break-even zone. These units have a net result between -5% and +5%, keeping their business more or less alive. The third and highest level of healthy units are those making a profit of more then 5%, on average. In figure 2.3 the net profitability, by type of activity is shown[10]. In Hosur-town 60% of all small-scale enterprises are in the first and second level. In the input sector the number of units in the 'danger-zone' is even higher (75%). The finished-product sector is in general operating more profitably, here two-third are making good or high profits. In fact, almost half of them even have profits of more then 15%. On the estates the profitability is, in general, higher. Of all units 70% are making a profit. More than half of them make profits of more than 15% on average. Surveying the picture so far, it is clear that the input sector in town is the least profitable. The small-scale units on the estates are of a larger scale in turnover and level of investment. They are in general also more profitable. The question now is if they are also more productive relatively in terms of capital and labor used.

Productivity

On the estates all units are of a 'modern' type of small-scale production, while in town there is a mix of 'modern' and 'traditional' types. A realistic comparison must be made between 'modern' small-scale and large-scale enterprises, since 'traditional' units are by nature labor-intensive. Nevertheless, it is clear that the small-scale units on the estates, being of larger-scale relative to town, are about three times more capital-intensive than units in town (see table 2.4). In recent research, by B. Harriss (1987), a calculation of capital intensity for two other industrial estates, in North-Arcot, is given. On the Katpadi-estate the mean total of investment is around Rs 6 lakh, which is between the average figures of town and the estates in Hosur. The capital intensity here is around Rs 26.000, which is

---

[10] The net profitability was calculated on the basis of turnover and the different cost categories.

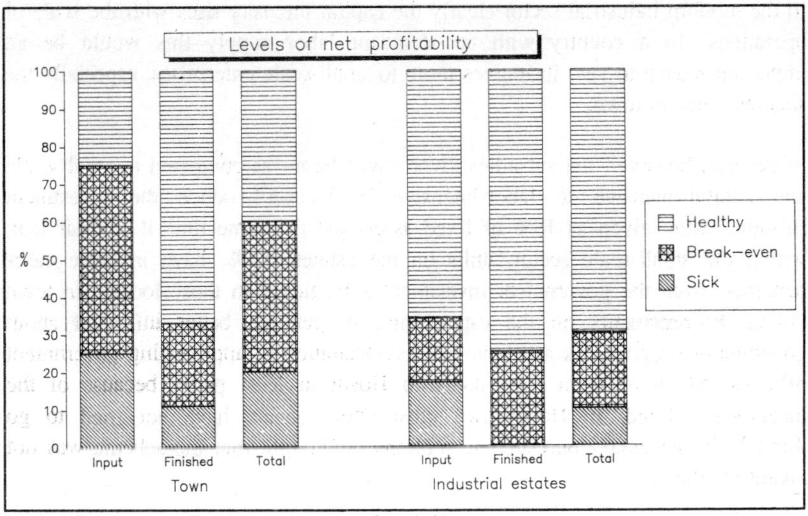

Figure 2.3 Net profitability by type of activity

also between that of town and the small-scale estates in Hosur. On the Ranipet estate, with relatively more larger-scale units, the capital intensity is higher: Rs 71.000. In Hosur the forty largest SIPCOT units have a capital intensity of, on average, Rs 123,000[11]. This is twice as large as the capital intensity on the SIDCO estates for small-scale units.

The Dharmapuri district has, by far, the highest capital intensity in the (larger-scale) factory sector in Tamil Nadu: Rs 115,000. The larger-scale sector in Hosur dominates the figures for the Dharmapuri district as a whole[12].

Table 2.4 Capital intensity[13]

	Town			SIDCO			SIPCOT
	input	finished	total	input	finished	total	
capital-intensity (x 1000 Rs)	21	13	18	61	66	63	123
	(n=16)	(n=8)	(n=24)	(n=7)	(n=5)	(n=12)	(n=40)

Source: own survey 1986.

[11] This estimate is based on figures concerning the number of employees in Meijer and Heins (1985) and initial investment levels as supplied by the SIPCOT-office. The capital intensity will, in reality, be higher since additional investments are not taken into account.

[12] Madras Institute of Development Studies (1988) Tamil Nadu Economy: Performance and Issues, p. 199, using data from 1982/83. The district of Madras occupies a second place with Rs 86,000 of fixed capital per worker.

[13] Capital intensity = present investment per Rs 1,000 divided by the total employment generated.

In the modern industrial sector clearly the capital intensity rises with the scale of operations. In a country with an abundant labor supply this would be an important reason to gear incentives more to small-scale enterprises, especially the smallest ones in town.

In general, however, the subsidies given favor large- as compared to small-scale and capital-intensive to labor-intensive production[14], since the investment subsidies were given as 15% of fixed assets. At the same time it is clear that, within the small-scale sector, units on the estates (84%) have in more cases benefited from the government investment subsidies than those located in town (14%). Entrepreneurs on the estates are, in general, better informed about government programmes and have far less hesitation in approaching government officials. Many of them have come to Hosur at least partly because of the incentives offered. In Hosur-town most entrepreneurs have not tried to go through the necessary bureaucratic motions or thought that the scheme was not meant for them.

2.2.2 The employees

The issue of the employees is of special importance. Firstly, because the growth of employment is one of the goals of the government policy. Secondly, but not less important, is the question of what kind of employment is offered.
The total employment accumulated in the small-scale (industrial) sector amounts to 2066 (607 in town; 1459 on the estates). In town the average number of employees is almost 6, on the estates it is around 14 (see table 2.5). In town in 85% of the units there are less than 10 employees.

Table 2.5 Number of employees classified, total and on average

	Town			Ind.Est.		
number	input	finished	total	input	finished	total
1 - 5	60%	58%	59%	17%	3%	13%
6 - 9	28%	24%	26%	19%	25%	21%
10 -25	11%	18%	14%	58%	63%	59%
26 - >	1%	-	1%	6%	9%	7%
	100% (n=65)	100% (n=38)	100% (n=103)	100% (n=69)	100% (n=32)	100% (n=101)
total	380	227	607	915	544	1,459
average	5.9	6.0	5.9	13.3	17.0	14.4

Source: own survey 1986.

The scale of operation is clearly larger on the estates, where in 66% of the units 10 or more employees are working. Officially, units with more than nine employees (and using power) have to register under the Factory Act. This

[14] See also Bharathan (1981).

registration means that the unit should obey certain regulations concerning minimum wages and safety. But, actually having more than nine employees does not automatically means that the unit is really registered. A common answer in the somewhat larger units to the question of the number of employees was 9. After convincing the entrepreneurs that I was in no way connected with the government apparatus, they usually came around and told me the actual number of employees. Only on the estates, 15% of the units were registered under the Factory Act. Other government registrations, apart from sales tax, are almost purely administrative, and do not mean that the unit cannot withdraw itself more or less from government control.

J. Harriss (1982) divides the labor market in urbanized areas in four main categories. The first are the permanent wage workers, protected by the Factory Act. The second category, the short-term wage workers, is sub-divided in two groups: temporary and contract workers, also protected by the Factory Act, and workers with a 'permanent' job in a small-scale unit, without legal protection. Then there are the casual wage workers, while the last category consists of the dependent and self-employed workers. Harriss (1986, p. 6) states that the division of the labor market: "... may be understood as different dimensions of vulnerability." .

All the employees in the small-scale sector in Hosur are part of the short-term wage workers without legal protection. Within this group there are again two distinctly different groups: those with in general a rather 'lasting' kind of employment and those hired on a more 'loose' basis[15]. Employees with a lasting type of short-term employment are usually the skilled workers who are indispensable for the ongoing of the production process. The maximum of security for the employees with a more lasting type of short-term employment appears to be a kind of mutual understanding: if his work is satisfactory, he can stay. The loose short-term employees are directly dependent on the regularity in performance. They are not paid when there is a flaw in orders, although they are usually re-hired once a new order comes through. None of the units, neither in town nor on the estates, have labor contracts with their employees. So, both types can be laid off on a day's notice.

In Hosur-town there are in the small-scale units about as many lasting as loose short-term wage workers (see figure 2.4). On the industrial estates, and especially in the finished product sector, the situation is different. The higher employment levels on the estates are mainly of a loose short-term nature. On the average of 16 employees in the finished-product sector there are 12 hired on a more loose basis.

The large number of loose short-term employees do usually not participate in the

[15] The entrepreneurs use the terms permanent and casual to describe the difference. These terms are however already used in the categorization by Harriss, 1982, for other groups of employees. The terms lasting and loose can be seen as an extension of the permanent/casual distinction within the category of the short term wage workers without legal protection. (For discussion about labor typologies, see 3.4.1).

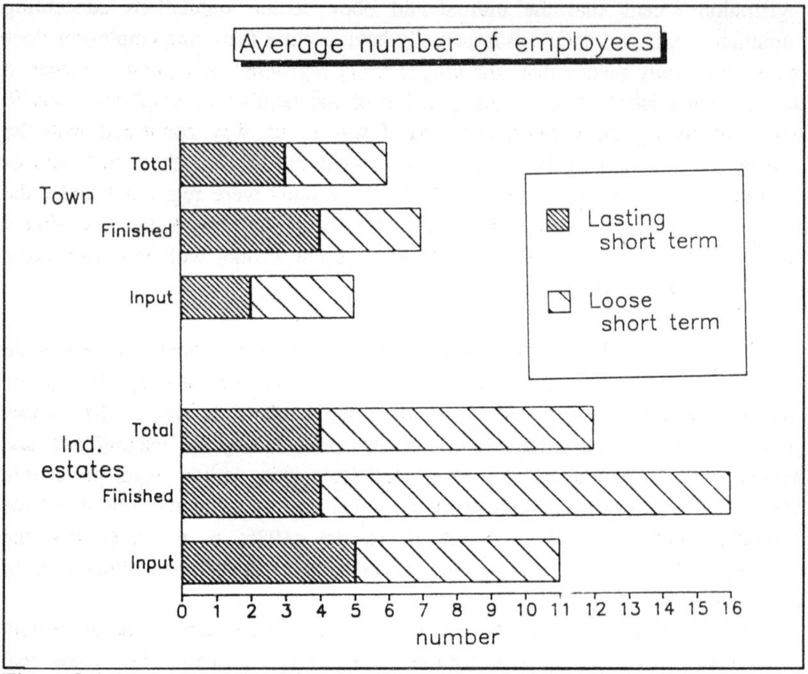

Figure 2.4 Average number of employees, total and divided by status (averages rounded to integers)

actual production process, but assist the skilled workers. The few women that work in the small-scale sector are mostly hired as such on the SIDCO estate. One extreme example of this is a manufacturer of (bubble-)gum. Here 5-6 skilled workers are taking care of the production, with partly imported machinery, while at times up to 60 girls wrap each piece of gum in a paper and a cellophane. When units have experienced growth in the last years this usually means that if extra employees are hired at all, they can primarily be found in the category of loose short-term employees.

Entrepreneurs do not have difficulties in finding new employees, except when they are looking for skilled workers. Then they face competition from the SIPCOT units. The wages at SIPCOT firms are higher, the working hours far more regular and an official labor contract possible especially for skilled workers. The average wage levels depend on the different skill levels. A skilled worker in the small-scale sector earns around Rs 700 a month. The unskilled workers between Rs 200 and Rs 250 a month, also depending on age. The wage levels in the small-scale sector are rather low when compared with the larger-scale sector[16]. At the same time they are reasonable or even high when compared with other groups in Hosur.

[16] See chapter 3.

2.2.3 Background entrepreneur

A theoretical division can be made between two types of entrepreneurs[17]: financiers ("white-collar") and technicians ("blue-collar"). During the study it became clear that a third category, those with a mixed background, had to be added. The typical financier comes from a 'white-collar'-family and most of them (78%) have a university degree, usually bachelor of commerce. Their experience is usually restricted to this area, as most of them are rather young. Their strength lies in marketing, establishing and maintaining the right contacts. The typical technician has a short general education. Roughly half of them acquired their technical knowledge completely through on-the-job training and experience while the other half also have some official technical schooling. They have worked their way up to skilled worker or supervisor in a larger-scale unit before they decided to start their own business. The entrepreneurs in the category 'mixed' usually have both technical and managerial experience. Many of them have spent some years in another country (mainly the Gulf) and/or worked for major companies. Since the running of a small-scale enterprise requires both technical and managerial skills, they appear to have the best starting position.

In town 64% of all entrepreneurs can be regarded as technicians (see figure 2.5). They operate mostly in the input sector (81%). Financiers in town are found mainly in the finished-product sector (56%). On the estates the number of entrepreneurs with a mixed background is highest (50%). Here, only one on every five entrepreneurs is a technician.

Panini, who did research on the Faridabad Industrial Estate, concludes that: "The style that succeeds is one which lays stress on building and articulating powerful networks." Whereby: "... a minimal capacity to manage and organize the firm is nevertheless essential." (1978, p. 114). Therefore, it is important to maintain good contacts with the purchasing officers of the larger-scale units. The social background of these managers is to a large extent comparable with that of the university-trained financiers and those with a mixed background. A few small-scale entrepreneurs are even members of the SIPCOT Lions Club Hosur, consisting primarily of managers of the larger-scale enterprises. Clearly a membership of this club improves the possibilities to obtain orders. The few small-scale entrepreneurs that are member of the Lions Club are financiers or from a mixed background. More in general they have an easier entry to managers, as compared with the technicians. A social 'gap' exists between the white and blue collar entrepreneurs[18].

---

[17] See Holmström (1984), p. 89-107 and Panini (1978).

[18] In this issue of course also the caste position of the different types of entrepreneurs is reflected very much.

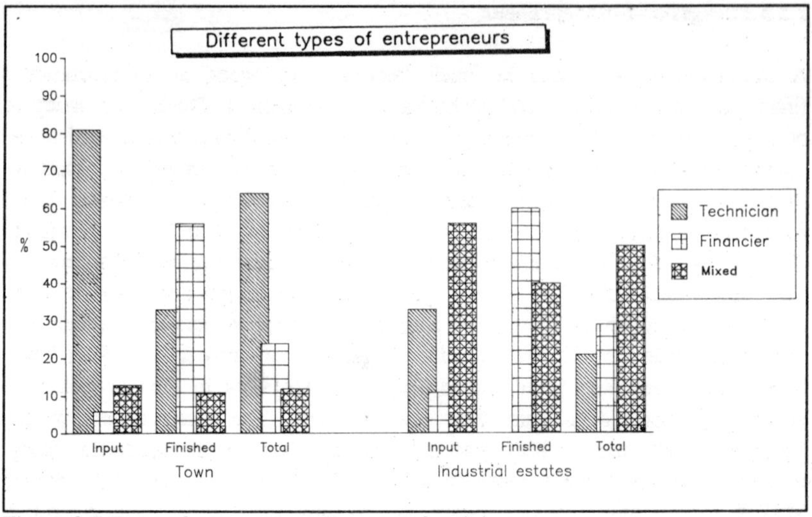

Figure 2.5 Type of entrepreneur by type of activity

This difference is also important in obtaining finance. In general, the most important source of initial investment are the, rather accessible, government loans. In town also non-institutional loans are important, especially in the 'traditional' finished-product sector. On the estates practically all units have institutional loans.

Working capital

Apart from the investment in shed, machinery etc., working capital is a prime necessity. Government loans are not given for working capital, so entrepreneurs have to depend on the nationalized banks for working capital. The nationalized banks are far more reluctant, especially to units in town, and their rates of interest are higher. Around half of the small-scale sector faces working-capital shortages, mainly units run by technicians. The somewhat larger units in town, and those on the estates, often have a demand-draft account at one of the nationalized banks. For those without this possibility there are the private money lenders, whose rates are far higher than those of the official financial institutions. Also friends and family are often called upon for small short-term loans to keep the unit running, together with, in some cases, the selling of personal possessions. Difficulties in acquiring finance for investment and working capital are experienced mainly by technicians operating in the input sector in town. The reason for the need of considerable working capital is that the larger-scale enterprises are slow in paying. In the input sector in town the average period that elapses between finishing the job and receiving the payment is around three months. The other units have to wait two months, on average. At the same time, the small-scale units usually have to pay their costs in cash. Complaining is difficult since it is very important for the small-scale entrepreneur to remain at least on speaking terms with the purchasing officers.

Results

An analysis of profits, as done in figure 2.3, can also be made of the different types of entrepreneurs, which shows clearly the differences in results (see table 2.6).

Table 2.6 Net profit as % of turnover for different types of entrepreneurs.

	technician	financier	both
sick	24%	11%	11%
break-even	52%	22%	11%
healthy	24%	67%	78%
	100% (n=17)	100% (n=9)	100% (n=9)
average %:	2.0%	15.3%	18.7%

Source: own survey 1986.

The technicians have by far the poorest results. Three out of every four of the technicians are either making a loss (24%) or can be found in the break-even-area (52%), just keeping the business alive. The situation of the financiers is quite different: two out of every three are making reasonable to very high profits. The entrepreneurs with a mixed background are doing even better: 78% of them is making a profit. Another way to show the differences in results is to show the average net profit. For technicians this is 2.0%, while for financiers the average is 15.3% and for those with a mixed background even 18.7%. This means that the differences in background of the entrepreneur are important in analyzing the differences in performance in the small-scale sector.

Since the labor market reflects different dimensions of vulnerability it is useful to see how the small-scale entrepreneurs fit into the classification made by Harriss. Apart from the division in different types of entrepreneurs two more indicators are used to determine their position in the labor market. Usually they are in principle self-employed but their self-employment is specifically chosen for, and not a last resource to try and make a living. Therefore, the first indication is their income level. Those earning more than Rs 1000 a month are labelled 'petit-bourgeois', as distinct from self-employed also by social status. Only in town one-third of the entrepreneurs earn less than Rs 1000[19], all of them technicians. The second indication is whether they participate in the actual production process. In that case they would at the same time be capitalist and worker. Pansters (1985) has typified them as not fully crystallized capitalists, since they still function predominantly as capitalists. This participation is highest

[19] Including possible additional income from other sources.

among technicians, where 58% works at least regularly in the actual production. Only 20% of the entrepreneurs with a mixed background and none of the financiers participate in the actual production process. In summing up it turns out that those earning less than Rs 1000, all of them technicians, are also at least regularly participating in actual production. This group, one-third of the entrepreneurs in town, can be considered as self-employed and not fully crystallized capitalists. In this group we also find the few real petty producers, who work permanently in actual production. They have, at most, one or two boys, extended family relations, assisting them and they operate, at first sight, somewhat outside the new industrial atmosphere. The other entrepreneurs in town and all of the entrepreneurs on the estates can be described as petit-bourgeois. According to Tyabiji, the political aim of the government of India's 'small industries policy' is: "... the creation of a class of small capitalist entrepreneurs." (Tyabiji 1984, p. 1425). If this would indeed be the main objective, the policy in Hosur can be called a success.

With this statement the section on the internal aspects of the small-scale sector can be concluded. We are now able to deal with the implications of the forward linkages on the performance of the small-scale sector in Hosur.

2.3 Forms of subcontracting

In the further analysis of the forward linkages the main focus will be on the input sector, subject to different forms of subcontracting. The first and most specialized group is that of the pattern-, die-, and tool-makers[20]. They manufacture important parts of the machinery used in the production process, that the larger-scale unit cannot manufacture itself. Their orders are based on the presence of specialized knowledge and they occupy a high position in the chain of subcontracting relationships. In Hosur this is only a small sub-sector of four units in town and four on the estates. None of them have difficulties in getting enough orders, because of an abundant demand. Units located in town get all their orders from the local larger-scale sector. The units on the estates also work for larger-scale units in Bangalore and Madras. The special feature of this industry is also shown in its giving out of job-works to other small-scale units. Although their strong bargaining position depends on specialized knowledge, this does not always involve the use of sophisticated machinery. In town there are two units that use hand-tools only. They make a masterpiece from teak-wood on the basis of drawings supplied. They also undertake the fine grinding of almost finished patterns or dies.

The second group are the manufacturers of 'normal' components who, on a subcontracting basis and with possible assistance (drawings etc.), manufacture the component, with raw materials they buy themselves. This group is somewhat larger (12.5% of the input sector in town; 50% on the estates). All of the units

[20] This sub-sector was not represented in the sample but examined separately.

on the estates in this group are making reasonable or high profits. This second group operates on a higher level of specialization than those doing rough job-work. The general feeling, however, among managers in the larger-scale sector is that the small-scale units in Bangalore and other major cities are more capable in terms of quality and delivery. At present, therefore, most of the orders requiring more specialized knowledge are given to units in Bangalore and Madras. Entrepreneurs in this part of the input sector are trying to convince the managers in the larger-scale sector of their capabilities. This is a difficult and slow process though some have succeeded in accomplishing it very well. Competition in this part of the input sector is heavy, but at least to some extent, its outcome is determined by the level of quality and the degree of specialization involved.

The largest group in the input sector (75% in town; 50% on the estates) consists of those engaged in job-works and labor-jobs for the larger-scale units. Among the sampled units in this sub-sector there was only one unit, on a total of eight, operating really profitable. This unit is run as a side-business by an entrepreneur with a 'mixed' background whose main job is manager in one of the largest SIPCOT units. Therefore, the issue of the right contacts does not pose any problems for him. All the other units are 'sick' or operating in the break-even zone. In the job-work sector the quality desired and delivered is far more standardized and can be undertaken with almost equal results by most units. It is especially in this sector where competition is fiercest because of the large growth in the number of such units. Therefore irregularity of incoming orders is a major problem. In town more then half of the input sector has less then 50% of its job-work coming in regularly. On the estates the situation is somewhat better (67%). The other units, both in town and on the estates, which have to cope with high irregularity, are all run by technicians.

The process of seeking orders in a highly competitive market can be witnessed in the waiting rooms of the purchasing officers. Here the small-scale entrepreneurs wait their chance. The purchasing officer exploits his bargaining strength in a number of ways. Quotations given are very low, conditions and time schedules very strict. There is an atmosphere of 'take it or leave it' and 'divide and rule'. There are certain purchasing officers in medium-scale units who use their bargaining power also for their personal benefit. A percentage (usually 10%) of the amount of the order has to be left at his disposal in order to assure a next 'load'.

The technicians are at a disadvantage in contacts with the purchasing officers and they are generally found in the job-work and labor-job sector. Taking also into account that they have to wait on average longest for their payments, and that there are no government loans for working capital, together with the fact that the nationalized banks are reluctant to give them additional loans, and a vicious circle is almost complete. There are many units in this sector facing difficulties and some have to close down. Nevertheless, there are, by far, more units starting up.

In the other sector and for other types of entrepreneurs the situation is better. In the finished-product sector competition is strong but the market is not yet overcrowded. They try to sell their products: cardboard boxes, crates, bill-books etc. to the larger-scale enterprises. When the growth in this part of the finished-product sector continues, overcrowding might however take place in a few years, unless the number of larger-scale enterprises in the area would grow accordingly. Financiers and entrepreneurs with a mixed background have, in general, a better access to orders and working capital. In general therefore, their bargaining position in the economic structure is better.

2.3.1 The subcontracting pyramid

Not all larger-scale enterprises incorporate subcontractors in their production. This is done mostly by units in the steel-based industries and is especially true for the two largest companies in the area: TVS and Ashok Leyland, producing a.o. transport equipment. The TVS group gives orders to 23% of the small-scale units. Ashok Leyland provides 18% with orders. Unfortunately, there are no data on the relative importance of the orders for either the small-scale sector or the larger-scale unit. Nevertheless, the numbers themselves are impressive and show some of the complexity of the Hosur industrial structure. Two examples of the linkages of a large and a medium scale unit in the metal-based sector will be presented. Firstly, the linkages of one of the units belonging to the TVS group and, secondly, a medium-scale unit on the SIPCOT estate.

The TVS unit is a supply industry for other companies in the same group. It manufactures components for automobiles, 2- and 3-wheelers and textile machinery. It is, therefore, also a typical example in the chain of more and less specialized phases in the production process of e.g. automobiles. This unit has a turnover of around Rs 5 crores, employing around 200 people and it collaborates with a (West-)German company. The total number of suppliers of all kinds of items is around 900 enterprises, large and small. These suppliers are widely spread throughout India and other countries. Around 40% of all suppliers are based in Bangalore, while around 9% of them are located in the Hosur area. This means around 80 suppliers, of which 35 are non-manufacturing units that supply services. The units in the manufacturing sectors are: 4 medium-scale units on the SIPCOT estate, 21 units on the SIDCO estates and 20 units in town; around 20% of all small-scale units in the area. If one looks at the kind of orders given, the picture is as follows. Of the total of 41 small-scale suppliers, 31 are in the input sector, mainly undertaking job-work. The other 10 are in the finished-product sector and supply printing items and packing materials.

The other example is a medium-scale unit on the SIPCOT estate manufacturing grinding wheels as its main activity. Their turnover is around Rs 8 crores, with 100 employees. This unit is part of a larger company, based in Madras, with a total turnover of around Rs 60 crores and 3000 employees. The unit gets it raw materials from another unit of the same company. Around 20% of their total workload is undertaken by small-scale units which they claim to be supplying on a regular basis. One specialized unit on SIDCO is manufacturing dies for them, two others make various components. There are also two units that take care of the repair and maintenance of the machinery. The other three units are in the job-work sector and their supply of orders is not regular.

These data show some of the interlinkages in the Hosur industrial structure. It is, e.g. rather likely that the 4 SIPCOT based suppliers of the TVS unit will pass at least part of their rougher work on to smaller units. This is certainly true for the SIDCO unit manufacturing dies. In the pyramid of subcontracting relationships the job-work sector is the lowest and most crowded level facing structural constraints. In theory there are two ways to deal with the problems the small-scale job-work units face: ancillarization or joining forces.

2.3.2 Ancillarization

The ancillary status is heavily debated among the small-scale entrepreneurs. The advocates point to the 'father-and-son' relationship that would 'nurture' the small-scale units and thus enable them to develop. Other entrepreneurs do not aspire the ancillary status. They feel that they would lose there independence by becoming an ancillary unit. It is however debatable if, in the present situation, their dependence is in reality smaller. The government policy stimulates ancillarization. As a guide-line the government policy mentions that around 40% of the workload of the larger-scale sector should be given to the small-scale sector. The government reports on this issue also mention that the well-being of small-scale ancillary units is, for a large part, the responsibility of the larger-scale sector. A unit is classified as ancillary unit when it is working for one major unit on a long term contract, receiving at least 50% of its workload from this large-scale unit. In Hosur-town 11% of the units in the input sector are more or less official ancillaries, on the estates even 23%. Ancillaries can be found on different levels of specialization. Conditions are mainly in favor of the larger-scale unit. The small-scale unit is not allowed to undertake other subcontracting or manufacturing work that might endanger the time schedule. In general, no firm assurances are given as to the size of the workload to be given to the small unit. Officially no ancillary can be a subsidiary of, or owned or controlled by, any other undertaking. This condition is included to prevent large industrial houses from exploiting the benefits meant for ancillary units. However, although these benefits might not be directly going to the large-scale sector at present, they will benefit indirectly. It is the larger-scale sector that can save tremendously on its costs by giving out job-works. Because of the present market situation also ancillaries are not able to secure reasonable quotations.

For small-scale units ancillarization means, also theoretically, the end of independence. If small-scale units, by long term contracts, become more or less subsidiary units there are no opportunities for independent growth. The small-scale unit will be completely subordinated to the large-scale sector. A more evenly distribution of economic power, one of the theoretical advantages of small-scale industrial development, does not occur in such a situation. If, however, the possible positive effects of ancillarization would be assured this process has certain important practical advantages. More regularity and technical assistance have been mentioned already. Growth in ancillary units will not be independent, but if the positive aspects are secured growth as such is more likely. Also, it might in the most optimistic view lead to a 'formalization' of these ancillary units. This could lead to an improvement in the situation of the employees if labor contracts are also 'formalized'. In that case their vulnerability would decrease. However, the main reason for larger-scale units to give out subcontracting work is that small-scale units can undertake those phases of production that require less specialization cheaper. They will therefore, in principle, be opposed to improvements in such less specialized small-scale units and employees in these units when this means higher costs. At present the ancillarization issue is used by larger-scale enterprises to improve their image of 'creators' of employment while neglecting its moral obligations to their ancillaries.

2.3.3 Joining forces

The second, and structural, way to improve the bargaining power of units in the input sector would be for them to form a block against the larger-scale units. They could determine some fixed rates for certain types of job-work, to make a divide-and-rule policy by the larger-scale units impossible. In principle this might be effective, since the larger-scale units are in a way also dependent on the small-scale sector. Part of the profits made in the larger-scale sector because of giving out part of the work, could then go to the small-scale units. There are three associations of small-scale enterprises in Hosur. At present, however, none of the associations acts as a pressure group against the larger-scale units in the area. And if they would act as such there are probably always enough units prepared to work 'under the price'. In view of the individualistic approach by most entrepreneurs in Hosur this alternative is not realistic.

2.4 Conclusions

A fine tuned division of tasks between different types of production units has evolved in the industrial structure of Hosur, which is dominated by metal based sectors. The small scale units are incorporated in the industrial structure through subcontracting or operate in the niches of the local and regional market. The larger-scale units on the SIPCOT estate are often linked to head offices in Bangalore and Madras and their production is overwhelmingly oriented towards the national and international markets.

In Hosur three estates have been set up. The majority of the factories are located on one of the estates, but several are located away from them. Two types of programmes are in operation to hasten industrial development. These programmes give financial incentives and provide physical infrastructure.

There has been extensive growth in the volume of production and employment in the large and small-scale sector in the past ten years. The bargaining position of the employees in the small-scale sector is, however, very weak; consequently, their vulnerability is high. The employees are informally employed, so there are no employees with labor contracts. The growth can be attributed to the establishment of larger-scale enterprises in the area because of the government policy. There is a trickle-down effect to small-scale industrial units in Hosur. Growth mainly comes from the increasing number of units in this sector, while growth within existing units is less important. Especially the increase in the number of units with strong linkages with the local larger-scale sector has been impressive in the last years.
The bargaining strength of small-scale units is, in general, rather slight, and this is especially true of units in the input sector. The fact that the local larger-scale sector is the main client, together with the strong competition accounts for the weak bargaining position. Mainly technician-entrepreneurs face difficulties in establishing the essential right contacts with the purchasing officers of the larger-scale units. An exception must be made for units operating on the basis of some kind of specialized knowledge. Taken as a whole, the growth in the small-scale sector, especially in town, will probably continue in the coming years. It must be noted that this means that the number of starting units will be higher then the number of units that fail. Data from the study indicate that at least 20% of the units in town and 10% of those on the estates can be called 'sick'. The units in difficulties are mostly found in the input sector. In the input sector in town, 25% make real losses, while another 50% is more or less keeping their business alive. At the same time, around 40% of the units in town and 70% of those on the estates are making good, or high, profits. This means that the units on the estates are far more profitable. In terms of generation of employment at a low cost of investment, the picture is reversed. Here the units in town create employment at a far lower level of investment. Since employment generation is an important goal of the government policy, this means that incentives should be geared more to small-scale units in town. Data, however, indicate that mainly units on the estates, large and small, have benefited from the government schemes. If the intention of the government policy has been to achieve economic growth as such, the policy can be called successful.

Lack of working capital is a serious constraint on growth faced especially by very small units and technician-entrepreneurs, since they have less access to financial institutions. Here, the government can play a role, by providing this working capital. Of course, this would be only a partial solution and a symptomatic approach.

Small-scale units producing finished products operate, in general, rather independently. Their prospects in a growing Hosur are in itself good. Small-scale units in the input sector are by nature dependent on larger-scale units for orders. Specialized small-scale units can obtain a reasonable independent position based on their bargaining strength. On the more standardized, and crowded, job-work level independence is not feasible. A 'true' ancillarization, with secured workload at reasonable prices and technical assistance, could solve their problems of irregularity in orders and lack of working capital. In the present circumstances, however, ancillarization is only to the benefit of the larger-scale sector. For small-scale units undertaking job-work the question is not whether ancillarization is desirable; but whether an ancillarization that is beneficial to them is feasible in today's India.

3. Population Mobility: the Migration and Commuting Process

Evert Meijer and Ko Heins

The expansion of economic activities in the last ten years has lead to considerable changes in the demographic structure of Hosur. This chapter will discuss the effects of the growth pole policy on population movements, both migration patterns and commuting. This is an important topic since one of the goals of the growth pole policy is involved. If the policy only benefits non-local immigrants while the local population does not take part in the growth, one can hardly speak of regional development.
The migration process will be studied by comparing Hosur with another small town in the Dharmapuri district: Krishnagiri. This town is located at a distance of 48 km from Hosur on the road to Madras, with 48,000 inhabitants in 1981. The growth rate in the seventies was a moderate 37%. Unlike Hosur hardly any industry has been set up in Krishnagiri, that traditionally is a commercial centre at the crossing of roads to Madras, Bangalore and Salem.

First we will pay some attention to the mobility theory for sake of definitions. The second paragraph focusses on migration, while commuting is dealt with in paragraph 3. The next paragraph concentrates on the labor structure of the different mobility groups. Finally conclusions are presented.

3.1 Definition of population movements

Population movements or territorial mobility can be defined as a movement of people from a place of origin to a place of destination at a certain distance. To structure the definitions the four crucial dimensions in conceptualizing territorial mobility from Standing (1982) are useful.
a. spatial criteria: mobility implies a movement from one place to another, thus the area has to be defined. In the present study all movements between towns and villages (administrative units) are recorded; intra-urban movements are thus excluded. This means that all people that have ever lived in another place than Hosur are regarded as a migrant.
b. temporal criteria: the reference period is the whole life of the respondent, in which all movements to other places that lasted longer than three months are recorded.

c. residence criteria: all persons that de facto live in a sample household are involved in the survey, except for visitors who stay less than 3 months.
d. activity criteria: a person can move place of activity without changing place of residence, as in the case of daily or weekly commuting, just as one can move place of residence without changing place of activity.

The first three criteria are concerned with migration patterns and will be discussed in paragraph 3.2 and 3.3. The last criterium on commuting needs some more attention at this place.
Commuters move to take up a specific activity, usually their economic activity, but retain their residence elsewhere. Commuting may be a substitute for different forms of residential movement (migration). Termote (1975) distinguishes three forms of commuting:

1. Commuting as a pure substitute for migration: commuting from place B to place A, reducing migration from B to A accordingly.
2. Commuting as a complement of migration:
   a. commuting from B to A by previous residents of A.
   b. commuting from B to A by previous residents of C who would otherwise have remained stationary.
   c. commuting from B to A by previous residents of C who would otherwise have migrated to A.
3. Commuting with neutral effect on migration: commuting from B to A by residents of B who would not have migrated in any case.

Data on the rate and incidence of commuting are remarkably scarce, except in a few industrialized countries. As far as we know no data on commuting[1] in India are available.

3.2 Migration

3.2.1 The data

In order to trace the effects of the growth pole policy, the migration to Hosur will be compared with migration data from the 1971 census. In the Census of India two types of migration data are distinguished:

1. life time migration: people born outside the place of enumeration are regarded as migrant. If a migrant has returned to his place of birth he is not

[1] In our survey we defined commuting with four criteria:
- the place of work is in Hosur town or the SIPCOT industrial area;
- the place of residence is at least 5 km outside Hosur (for the SIPCOT workers not within 5 km from the factory);
- the work is done at least three days a week
- the work takes at least 4 hours a day in Hosur / SIPCOT

Any person that fullfils all criteria has been defined as a commuter.

identified as a migrant.

2. last residence migration: the migrants are classified according to their last place of residence.

In the Census 1971 publications only data on district level are presented; it is not possible to get information on a lower level. In order to trace migration effects of growth pole policy, it was necessary to collect new data[2].

3.2.2 Hosur versus Tamil Nadu

The spatial characteristics concerning the 'place of origin' of the migrant and the 'distance' over which he/she moved to the current place of residence, are dealt with first. After that the duration of residence, a temporal characteristic, will be discussed.

In table 3.1 the census data on life time migration to urban areas in Tamil Nadu are compared with the survey-data in Hosur. The migration rate is in Tamil Nadu slightly lower than in whole India: 35.2% versus 39.3% of the population has been born outside the place of enumeration.

The situation in Hosur is quite different from whole Tamil Nadu, as could be expected. Not only is the migration rate much higher, but also the distribution among the places of origin differs.

The migration from rural areas in the Dharmapuri district to Hosur is relative low. This does not mean that the surrounding rural areas supply less migrants than elsewhere in the state: if the intra-district rural migration is measured as percentage of the total population in the destination urban area, the differences are small (10.0% in Hosur versus 11.3% in Tamil Nadu).

The migration from urban areas elsewhere in the State and from urban areas in other states is exceptionally high. It is immediately clear that the fast growth of Hosur in recent years is caused by in-migration from other urban areas, mainly outside the district. The sexe division is also quite different from the Tamil Nadu situation. In the whole state the female outnumber the male in intra-district migration and participate slightly less in the other types of migration. In Hosur the intra-district migration from rural areas is equal among men and women, while the migration from urban areas elsewhere in the State is dominated by men. Remarkable is the higher migration of women from (urban areas in) other states compared to men.

---

[2] The built-up area of Hosur has been subdivided, mostly according to main routes. From each part a sketch-map of the streets and lanes has been made, after which the number of households could be established by counting the number of doors. Though the result of this procedure is not the exact number of households, it does give a reasonable framework for drawing the sample of 200 households (2.5%). In each of the sampled households information on the migration history of all members has been gathered.

Besides the lifetime-migration data the census publications offer information on migration according to the last place of residence. In general there are not many differences in the distribution of migration types between both definitions. In figure 3.1 the percentage distribution of the migration types of the Dharmapuri district and Hosur are presented.

Table 3.1 Life time migration in Hosur (1985) and Tamil Nadu (1971)

		HOSUR 1985			TAMIL NADU 1971 urban pop.		
		male	female	total	male	female	total
Non-migrants		50.1%	51.7%	50.7%	67.9%	62.6%	64.8%
Migrants		49.9%	48.3%	49.3%	32.1%	37.4%	35.2%
Type of migration:							
Intra-district	RURAL	20.8%	19.7%	20.3%	29.3%	34.7%	32.1%
	URBAN	8.5%	12.7%	10.2%	10.1%	12.0%	11.1%
Inter-district	RURAL	10.0%	8.1%	9.2%	21.9%	18.1%	19.9%
	URBAN	42.7%	28.3%	37.0%	22.3%	21.9%	22.1%
Inter-state	RURAL	3.1%	8.7%	5.3%	6.2%	4.4%	5.2%
	URBAN	15.0%	22.5%	18.0%	8.4%	7.2%	7.8%
Outside India (incl unclassified)		.0%	.0%	.0%	1.9%	1.7%	1.8%
TOTAL		100.0%	100.0%	100.0%	100.0%	100.0%	100.0%
		(260)	(173)	(433)	(2,113)	(2,272)	(4,385)
			(* 1000)			(* 1000)	

Source: Census of India 1978; own survey 1985.

The short distance migration within the district from rural areas is in Dharmapuri higher than in whole Tamil Nadu, as is the inter-district migration from urban areas. Hosur is different from Dharmapuri in that the 'short-rural' migration is much lower, and even less than in whole Tamil Nadu, while the inter-district migration from urban areas is higher than in Dharmapuri (that itself is already substantial compared to Tamil Nadu).

3.2.3 Before and after 1975

The migration thus far described has not yet been differentiated according to the second main definition criterium, the temporal criterium. The growth pole policy started in the second part of the seventies, so it can be expected that the migration pattern in the last decennium is even more pronounced. For this reason in figure 3.2 the migration to Hosur before and after 1975 is shown, separate for the Dharmapuri district, bordering districts (North Arcot, South Arcot and Salem), Madras, the rest of Tamil Nadu, Bangalore and other places in India. The urban areas are divided into towns and cities (more than 100.000 inhabitants). Very clear is the enormous growth of migration from cities in Tamil Nadu, not only from the metropole Madras but also from other cities. Before 1975 only 3 migrants in the sample have come from the cities Madras, Salem and Coimbatore. After 1975 40 migrants have come from Madras, while cities like Coimbatore (17), Vellore (15), Tiruchchirappalli (8), Madurai (8), Salem (6) and Thanjavur (6) are other important cities of origin.

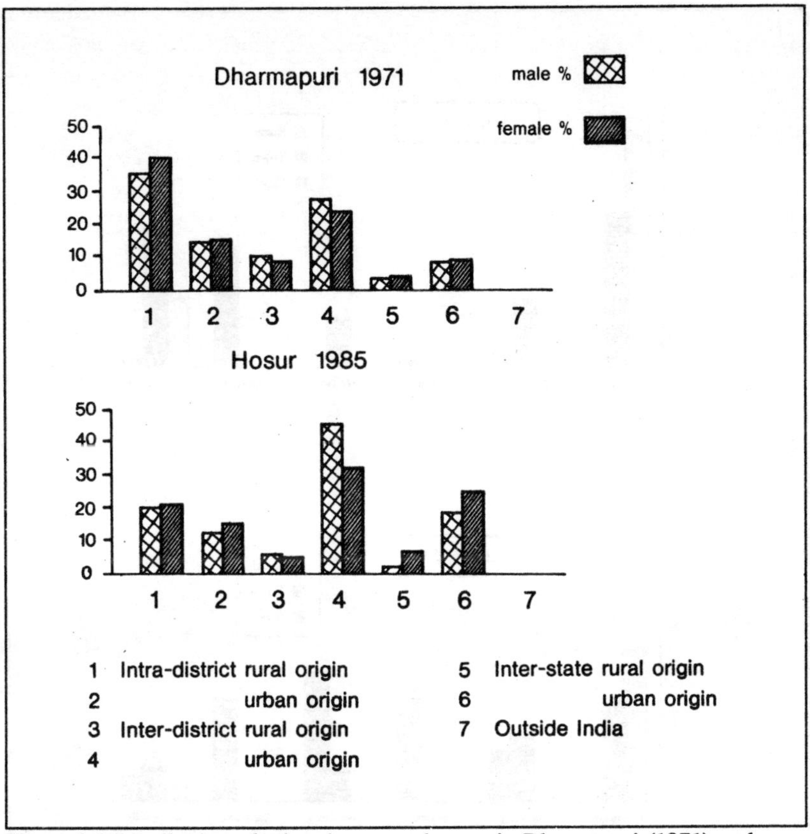

Figure 3.1 Distribution of migration types by sex in Dharmapuri (1971) and Hosur (1985) (source: own survey 1985)

Though the current intra-district migration accounts for an important part of the total in-migration (29%), it is relatively less substantial than before 1975. The number of migrants from the surrounding areas, coming to Hosur to find a job in the activities arisen as a consequence of the industrial development, is small. The indirect migration effects of the growth pole policy are thus minor.

3.2.4 Migration history

Census data do not give information on the exact place of origin, only the type of place (rural/urban) is reported. Also the number of moves and type of place(s) before the last place of residence are not available in the Census.

The migration history of the migrants to Hosur is analyzed by making a comparison with data from another town (without growth pole policy). As mentioned before, Krishnagiri has been chosen as 'control place'. Not all types

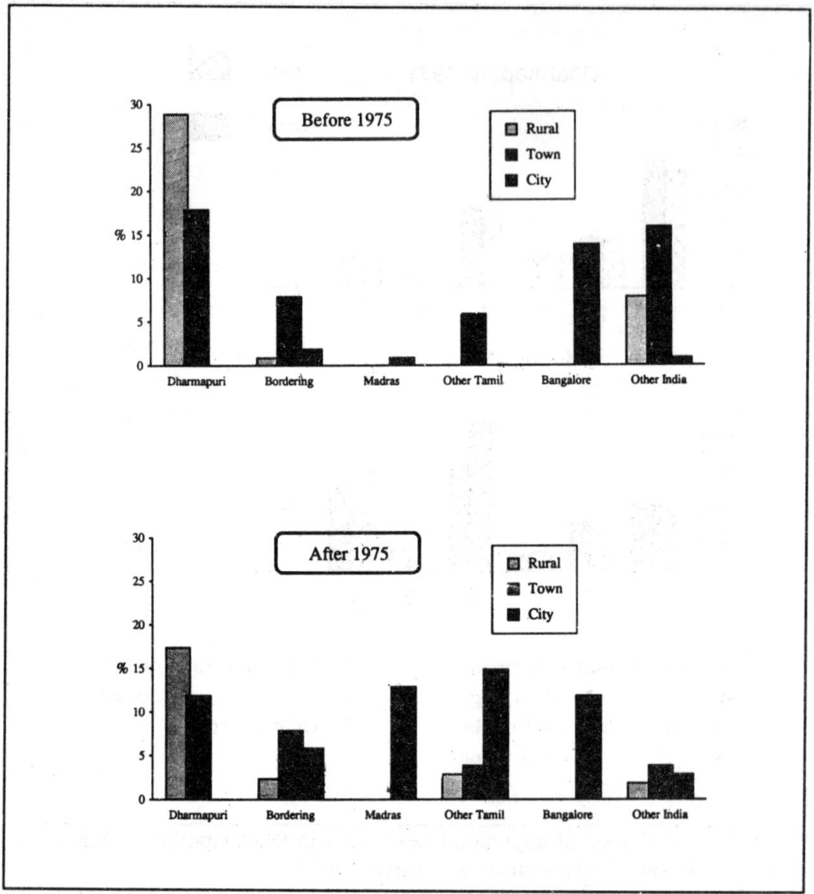

Figure 3.2 Migration to Hosur by last place of residence, arrived before and after 1975 (source: own survey 1985)

of migration are as relevant for our study. Children that come with their parents and women migrating to the place of their husband form migration processes that can hardly be influenced by policy measures. Therefore we selected the migration background of the heads of household for further analysis. For both places table 3.2 shows the places of origin of these migrants.

The percentage of migrant households is in Hosur almost twice the rate of Krishnagiri. Dharmapuri and the bordering districts play a more important role in the migration to Krishnagiri than to Hosur, where the migration from the metropoles Madras and Bangalore is substantial. It can be concluded that the distance over which the migration has taken place is in Hosur greater than in Krishnagiri.

Table 3.2 Migration to Hosur and Krishnagiri (heads of household only)

Last place of residence	Hosur abs	Hosur %	Krishnagiri abs	Krishnagiri %
Dharmapuri	45	31.9	31	42.5
Bordering distr.	23	16.3	22	30.1
Madras	15	10.6	4	5.5
Other Tamil Nadu	28	19.9	8	11.0
Bangalore	17	12.1	3	4.1
Other India	13	9.2	5	6.9
Rural	37	26.2	19	26.0
Town	43	30.5	29	39.8
City	61	43.3	25	34.2
TOTAL	141	100.0	73	100.0
Origin unknown	5		8	
Non-migrant households	52		120	
Migration rate	71.2		36.5	

Source: own survey 1985.

Another aspect of the migration history is the type of places the migrants have lived in. It is remarkable that the differences between the type of place of origin are much smaller. The rural migrants are equally represented in both places, while the towns and cities have changed position, the cities being more important as a supplier of migrants to Hosur.

Not all migrants have come directly from their birthplace to Hosur or Krishnagiri. Apart from the analysis of the last place of residence, it is interesting to see whether the complete migration history of the migrants to Hosur differs from other places. The number of migrants is too small to differentiate between all kind of combinations, for that reason in table 3.3 only the type of the last two places are taken into account.
The number of migrants that came directly from their place of birth to both places is slightly greater in Krishnagiri than in Hosur. This is caused by migrants

Table 3.3 Migration background of migrants to Hosur and Krishnagiri (heads of household)

background	Hosur abs	Hosur %	Krishnagiri abs	Krishnagiri %
rural	28	19.3	14	19.2
town	25	17.2	18	24.7
city	23	15.9	11	15.1
rural-rural	7	4.8	2	2.7
rural-town	8	5.5	4	5.5
rural-city	8	5.5	4	5.5
town -rural	1	0.7	3	4.1
town -town	8	5.5	5	6.9
town -city	12	8.3	6	8.2
city -rural	2	1.4	1	1.4
city -town	1	0.7	1	1.4
city -city	22	15.2	4	5.5
Total	145	100%	73	100%

Source: Own survey 1985.

from towns, as the 1-step migrants from rural areas and cities are equally represented in both places. The origin of the 2-(or more)step migrants shows generally the same pattern. Only the migrants that have been living in two cities before their present place are more found in Hosur, while the migrants that came from rural areas after having been in a town is somewhat greater in Krishnagiri.

Next we will take a look at all moves that have taken place before the migrants have arrived in the present town. In table 3.4 the places of origin and destination are divided into rural areas, towns and cities and the number of moves between them is given. Most striking is the difference between the number of city-to-city moves in both places: in Hosur it accounts for almost 28% of all moves, while in Krishnagiri it is 10% less (but still the most important type of move). In general, the number of moves originating in rural areas is not very different between both places, while the type of origin 'town' and 'city' have interchanged places. The moves with origin in towns are more common among the Krishnagiri-migrants, but their distribution among places of destination is about the same as for the Hosur-migrants. The place of destination is in Hosur more city-oriented.

Finally two figures have been calculated to take into account the whole migration history: the percentage of migrants who have never lived in a city and those who have never lived in rural areas. In Hosur these figure are 48.6% and 56.9%, in Krishnagiri respectively 51.3% and 56.6%, showing very little difference between the two towns.

Table 3.4 Type of moves before coming to Hosur and Krishnagiri (heads of household onl

	Hosur DESTINATION				Krishnagiri DESTINATION			
ORIGIN	rural	town	city	TOTAL	rural	town	city	TOTAL
rural	18 (9.7%)	16 (8.6%)	22 (11.9%)	56 (30.3%)	8 (9.6%)	8 (9.6%)	7 (8.4%)	23 (27.7%
town	9 (4.9%)	21 (11.4%)	23 (12.4%)	53 (28.6%)	7 (8.4%)	13 (15.7%)	12 (14.5%)	32 (38.6%
city	10 (5.4%)	15 (8.1%)	51 (27.6%)	76 (41.1%)	4 (4.9%)	9 (10.8%)	15 (18.1%)	28 (33.7%
TOTAL	37 (20.0%)	52 (28.1%)	96 (51.9%)	185 (100%)	19 (22.9%)	30 (36.1%)	34 (41.0%)	83 (100%)

Source: own survey 1985.

Duration of residence

The last part of this paragraph will pay attention to a temporal characteristic of migration: the duration of residence. How long have the migrants already lived in Hosur? This is an important question since it can give information about the permanency of the growth pole effect. If the migrants only come for a short time, earning some money to leave as soon as is needed for e.g. the education of the children, the effects for the local economy are different from the situation where migrants really settle in the growth pole. Table 3.5 compares the duration

of residence of the heads of household in Hosur with Krishnagiri. The period since the start of the growth pole policy is clearly reflected in these figures. About 10 years ago the large scale migration to Hosur started, resulting in a majority of migrants living in Hosur for less than 10 years (71%). In Krishnagiri most of the migrants (68%) have come before 1975.
No information is available concerning migrants who have left since their arrival in Hosur. But the fact that the time of arrival is rather evenly spread during the last years, gives an indication that migrants stay longer than only a very short period.

Table 3.5 Duration of residence of heads of household

	Hosur abs	Hosur %	Krishnagiri abs	Krishnagiri %
upto 1 year	9	6.2	3	3.7
1 - 2 year	9	6.2	1	1.2
2 - 4 year	43	29.5	7	8.6
5 - 9 year	43	29.5	15	18.5
10 - 19 year	21	14.4	26	32.1
20 +	21	14.4	29	35.8
TOTAL	146	100.0	81	100.0

Source: own survey 1985.

It can be concluded that the migration pattern to both towns shows some differences. The magnitude of the migration stream is in Hosur higher than in Krishnagiri, but distribution of the migrants among the different types of migration is roughly the same, except that Hosur attracts more migrants from cities, whereas Krishnagiri has more migrants coming from towns. The distance over which the migration has taken place is in Hosur considerably greater. The duration of residence clearly reflects the start of the growth pole policy.

3.2.5 Characteristics of the migrant households

The above data concern the type of moves the migrants have made before coming to Hosur, in this paragraph we will analyze the characteristics of the migrant households. They are compared with the migrants to Krishnagiri and the non-migrants in both places. Firstly the type of household that the migrants have formed will be discussed, secondly the education of the heads of household and finally the income.

Out of the 419 migrants to Hosur 123 or 29% are head of household[3], 66 (16%) lived together with friends as bachelors[4], while the other migrants are mostly wife (27%) or child (22%).

[3] The head of household is the person who is considered as such by the respondent.

[4] In paragraph 3.2.4 where the migration of heads of households is analyzed, one of the bachelors in a household is regarded as the head.

In table 3.6 the household types in Hosur and Krishnagiri by the migrant status of the head of the household are given. In all groups the householdtype 'couple with at least one child below the age of 15' is most important. The nuclear family without children younger than 15 is underrepresented among the migrants, as could be expected: migrants are in general younger, thus not yet having older children. In Hosur the number of extended families was expected to be lower than in Krishnagiri, as a consequence of the more 'modern' migrants. This is indeed the case, in both places the share of extended families among the non-migrants is in nearly all cases higher than among the migrants.

Composition of the population

The enormous influx of migrants has had considerable effects on the age-structure of the population of Hosur. Figure 3.3 represents the population pyramid of Hosur and Krishnagiri. The picture is quite clear: in Hosur the age-groups 20-35 are overrepresented, especially the male, as a consequence of the recent influx of young migrants. The older people and children between 10 and 20 years old are underrepresented. The 0-5 aged children already outnumber this age group in Krishnagiri. It can be expected that the high number persons between 20 and 35 in Hosur will cause a fast growth of the number of children.

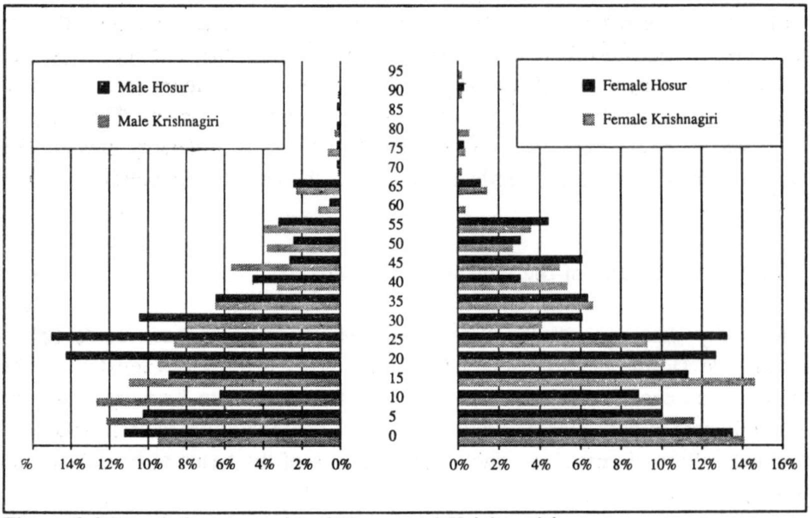

Figure 3.3 Population pyramid of Hosur and Krishnagiri

Special for Hosur is the phenomenon of bachelors living together. It concerns mostly young men coming from big cities (73%, especially Madras) for work in the industrial estates. They prefer to share a house for social and economic reasons. Slightly less than half of the bachelors live in the older parts of Hosur, but an increasing number of them lives in recently built housing schemes of the Tamil Nadu Housing Board where the standards of living are relatively high.

The high rent will not be a problem since they have rather high salaries at Sipcot and they can share the rent.

Table 3.6 Householdtype migrants and non-migrants in Hosur and Krishnagiri (%)

	Hosur		Krishnagiri	
	migrant	non-mig.	migrant	non-mig.
couple with child. < 15	47.3	38.5	46.4	41.4
couple with child. > 15	7.5	19.2	15.5	6.9
extended fam. with child. <15	10.3	28.8	22.6	36.2
extended fam. with child. >15	8.2	5.8	7.1	7.8
bachelors	13.7	0	0	0
other	13.0	7.7	8.3	7.8
total	100.0 (146)	100.0 (52)	100.0 (84)	100.0 (116)

Source: own survey 1985.

3.3 Commuting

3.3.1 The data

Information on commuting has been gathered in different ways. On the SIPCOT/SIDCO industrial area all big companies and a subset of the smaller ones have been visited to get information on the number of employees and the commuters among them. From this inventory we learned that, contrary to our expectations rather few of the employees lived outside Hosur (8%). According to the place of residence of the commuter (distance from Hosur and direction) a stratified sample has been interviewed.

To get information on the commuters to Hosur-town the above procedure was not possible. Originally we concentrated on the bus stand to catch the commuter when he/she leaves Hosur, expecting that most of them would go by bus. Practically this was not a fruitful manner: the crowd and time pressure when the buses leave made the response less reliable. Only a few of the sometimes more than 100 people in a bus seemed to be commuter. An alternative method was found in selecting a number of main streets in Hosur and visit all places of work (shops, streetsellers, workshops, etc.) to establish the number of workers and the number of commuters. This means that we do not have a complete picture of all types of commuters in town: those working outside the city center and those without a fixed place of work are not represented in the sample.
In this way we gathered information on 250 commuters; slightly more than half of them worked on the industrial area, the other part in Hosur-town. In table 3.7 an overall view of the number of commuters in the different samples is given.

Table 3.7 Commuters to Hosur and SIPCOT/SIDCO-area

	Hosur-town	SIPCOT	Bus stand
places of work	502	39	
employees/workers	1397	8432	
commuters	114	541	47
% commuters	12.3%	8.0%	
# in sample	114	103	34

Source: own survey 1985.

3.3.2 Characteristics of the commuting movement

The places of residence of the commuters have been classified in two ways: according to the size and to the distance from Hosur. The places with less than 3000 inhabitants in 1971 (the last available census data on this level) are regarded as villages, places with more than 3000 belong all to the category small towns[5]. Bangalore is treated separately as metropolitan. The distance is divided into five categories (see table 3.8).

Table 3.8 Percentage of commuters by distance from Hosur and size of place of residence compared with the population (1971) of Hosur and Denkanikotta taluk

size of place of residence	distance from Hosur in km 5 - 10	10 - 15	15 - 20	20 - 25	25 >	Total	
Commuters							
Village	7.5	1.5	1.0	0.5	4.0	14.4%	
Small town	18.9	3.5	11.4	16.4	8.5	58.7%	
Metropolitan					26.9	26.9%	
Total	26.4%	5.0%	12.4%	16.9%	39.3%	100 %	= 201
Population in Hosur and Denkanikotta taluk							
Village	8.6	7.8	22.0	13.1	17.3	69.1%	
Small town	1.7	0.9	5.8	7.9	14.7	31.0%	
Total	10.1%	8.6%	27.5%	20.8%	31.8%	100 %	= 340

Source: own survey 1985.

If we look at the places of residence of the commuters we find that nearly 60% comes from small and intermediate towns. Compared to the distribution of the total population in the area round Hosur, the small towns are strongly overrepresented. Only 14% travels daily from the villages and the rest is descended from Bangalore. The main part of the commuters from the villages lives very nearby Hosur, though some commute over a distance of more than 25 km. The commuters from small towns are more evenly spread over the distance classes. This is of course connected with the geographical distribution of this type of towns.

[5] We expected that the places of 3000 inhabitants in 1971 reached the limit of the definition of a town (5000) in 1986.

3.3.3 Residential preferences of the commuters

It is for planning purpose very interesting to know whether the commuters would like to reside in Hosur in the future and to analyze the main factors that influence the potential migration behavior of the commutersgroup.
In table 3.9 one can find the willingness of the different 'labor'groups to live in Hosur.

Table 3.9 Labor structure and willingness to reside in Hosur

	does not want	does want, no plans	does want, and plans	
permanent high	82.5	5.3	12.3	100% (57)
permanent low	73.2	7.3	19.5	100% (82)
short-term wage	70.0	12.9	17.1	100% (70)
casual wage	85.7	14.3	.	100% (7)
dep. and self-empl.	46.4	10.7	42.9	100% (28)
petit bourgeois	62.5	.	37.5	100% (8)
Total	71.4 (180)	8.7 (22)	19.8 (50)	100% (252)

Source: own survey 1985.

In the first place we can conclude that an important majority does not like to reside in Hosur. In particular the high-income, long-distance commuters from Bangalore are satisfied with their present residence. A small group of short-term wage workers likes to move to Hosur, but has no concrete plans. From the different labor groups the self-employed have the highest willingness to migrate.
If we look to the ages of the commuters we see that 58% of the youngest age groups (below 20 years) does not want to migrate to Hosur. The older age groups (in particular from 20 to 40 years) have relatively a more positive attitude with regard to a permanent stay in Hosur.
The most mentioned reasons that influence the decision (not) to move to Hosur are housing, family circumstances and cost of living. Less important factors are education, water and (health-)facilities. In particular housing is very important. Because of the own house in the present residence a lot of commuters are not willing to move to Hosur. The attachment to the family is in particular for the younger commuters an important reason not to settle in Hosur. The main obstacle for commuters who like to migrate, forms the housing problem. There are too few houses available and the rents are too high.

3.4 Characteristics of the migrants, commuters and non-migrants compared

In this paragraph we will discuss the characteristics of the commuters. Firstly attention will be paid to the labor structure. Secondly an analysis will be made of the geographical background of the commutersgroup. Lastly we make a comparison of some of the personal characteristics of the commuters, the migrant and non-migrant group in Hosur.

3.4.1 Labor structure

Several authors have proposed frameworks for the analysis of urban labor markets. In a study of Bromley and Birkbeck (1988) a more refined classification of economic activities has been developed (see figure 3.4). Rather than simply dividing workers' employment into two basic categories, 'wage work' in which employees work for employers, and 'self-employment', in which individuals work independently on their own account, there is a continuum of employment relationships which can be subdivided in terms of two major variables, 'relative stability and security of work opportunities', and 'relative autonomy and flexibility of working regimes and conditions'.

The two extremes of the continuum have relatively high levels of stability and security, and are described as 'career wage work' and 'career self-employment', while the various intermediate relationships have relatively low levels of stability and security and are described collectively as 'casual work'.

Casual work can be crudely divided into four broad categories: 'short-term wage work', 'disguised wage-work', 'dependent work', and 'precarious self-employment'.

Recently J. Harriss, K.P. Kannan and G. Rodgers (1990) carried out a (duplicate) research on the labor markets in Coimbatore. The authors made a new concept of the 'labor status', which is in line with the thoughts of Bromley and Birkbeck (1988). The 'labor status' is composed of the elements 'protection', 'autonomy'

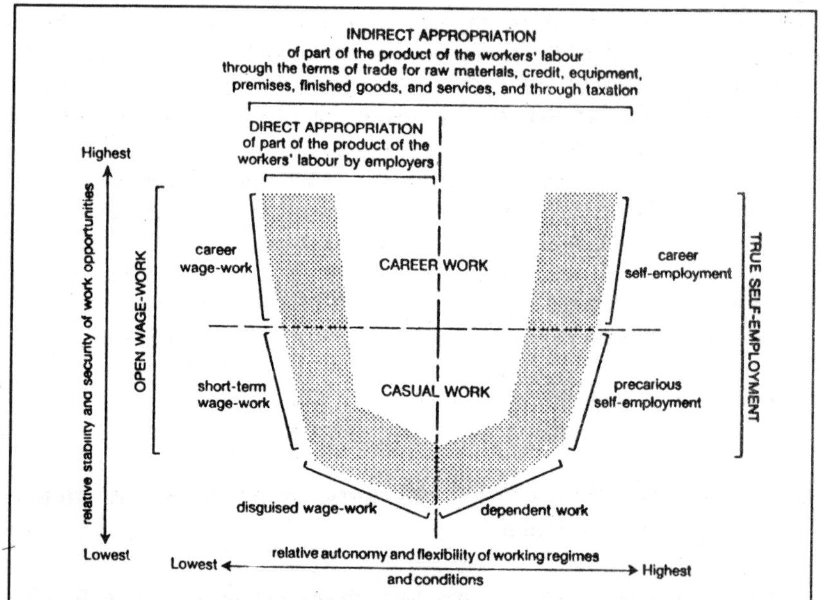

Figure 3.4 The continuum of employment relationships
(Bromley and Birkbeck 1988)

and 'regularity'. The category 'protection' (protected/unprotected) is the same as 'career and casual work' of Bromley's and Birkbeck's typology. They also take into account the 'autonomy' of the laborers. The third element of Harriss' typology is 'regularity' and is new compared to Bromley and Birkbeck. At each distinguished group of Bromley and Birkbeck can be added 'regularity'. A more refined categorization will appear.
The three components of the labor status may also be seen as dimensions of the 'vulnerability' of different groups of workers. Harriss remarks the strength and at the same time the weakness of his approach. The framework of the typology is strongly based on the own insights of the workers of their labor status. The terms 'permanency', 'autonomy' and 'regularity' will not have the same meaning for the workers all over the world, but at the contrary it makes clear the own perception of the workers at their labor status.

3.4.2 Labor structure and geographical background of commuters

In table 3.10 the geographical background of the commuters and their labor structure is presented. Most of the richer permanent wage workers travel each day more than 25 km. The short-term workers live relatively close to Hosur: more than 50% of this group does not commute from places further than 15 km distance. The self-employed people come frequently from places between 15-25 km. More than 80% of the richer permanent wage workers commute, mainly by company buses, from Bangalore. They dominate completely the long-distance commuting. There is a relatively strong overrepresentation of short-term wage workers who come from the small villages (nearly 30%).

The average income of each of the distance categories shows that in general the short-distance commuters are poorer than the long-distance ones (see the lower part of table 3.10). The income position of the commuters differs strongly dependent of the size of the place of residence.

Table 3.10 Distance place of residence, labor structure of commuters and income

size of place of residence	distance from Hosur in km					
	5 - 10	10 - 15	15 - 20	20 - 25	25 >	Total
permanent high	14.0	3.5	1.8	5.3	75.4	100% (57 = 22.9%)
permanent low	33.3	4.9	12.3	19.8	29.6	100% (81 = 32.5%)
short-term wage	44.9	11.6	17.4	8.7	17.4	100% (69 = 27.7%)
casual wage	42.9	14.3	.	42.9	.	100% (7 = 2.8%)
dep. and self-empl.	32.1	10.7	21.4	25.0	10.7	100% (28 = 11.2%)
petit bourgeois	42.9	.	28.6	.	28.6	100% (7 = 2.8%)
Total	32.5	7.2	12.4	14.1	33.7	100% (249)
Average income in Rs	545	546	705	618	1614	932

Source: own survey 1985.

3.4.3 Commuters, migrants and non-migrants compared

The expanding labor market in Hosur has given new opportunities to the traditional population of the town and to the new influx of migrants and commuters from outside. In figure 3.5 one can find the participation/position of the different local and non-local groups in the labor structure.
Only 31% of the labor force of the non-migrant group has access to the more attractive jobs in the modern factories. The main activities of this autochthonous group are connected with short-term wage labor, casual work and different forms of self-employment. It strikes that short-term wage labor plays an important role in the labor structure of the commuters, while self-employment is less important for this group.

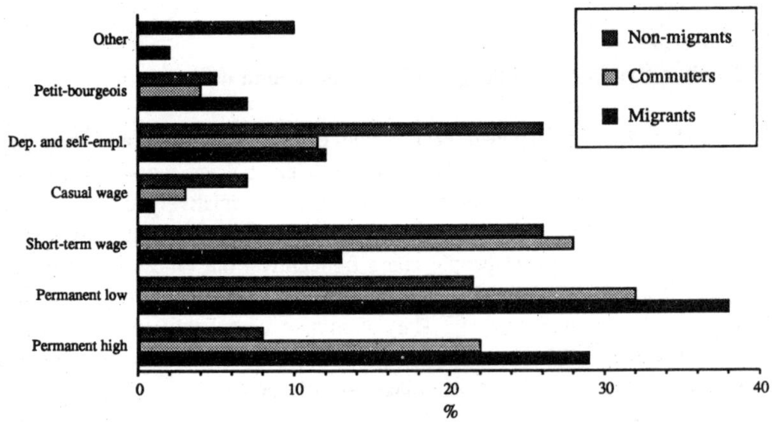

Figure 3.5 Labor structure of commuters, migrants and non-migrants in Hosur(*)

* For comparison between the commuter-survey and the migration data, we have taken a sample from all the economically active members of the households of the migration survey. At random we selected one member from every household.

In table 3.11 we present the age structure of the three (im)mobility groups. Nearly half of the commuter group belongs to the age group 20-29 years, while the migrant group is overrepresented in the 30-39 category and underrepresented in the youngest age groups. 30% of the non-migrants belong to the oldest age-categories.

In the next section we will pay attention to the income structure of the three groups.

Table 3.11 Commuters, migrants and non-migrants and their age

	commuters	migrants	non-migrants
10 - 19 years	8.1	2.2	8.6
20 - 29	46.7	33.6	36.2
30 - 39	32.1	41.7	25.9
40 - 49	11.0	13.9	17.2
50 -	2.0	8.8	13.0
Total	100.0 (251)	100.0 (137)	100.0 (58)

Source: own survey 1985.

The rise of formal and informal income opportunities has led to a differentiated income structure of the working population in Hosur (see table 3.12). The non-migrants form by far the poorest group; nearly 60% has an average income of less than Rs 500. A complete opposite position is taken by the migrants. 40% of them earns more than Rs 1000 and an important part raises even the highest incomes. The commuters are in particular represented in the lower middle-income categories. An important minority receives very high incomes.

Table 3.12 Individual and total household monthly income in Rs

Rs	individual income (%)			total household income (%)		
	commuters	migrants	non-migr.	commuters	migrants	non-migrants
0 - 249	8.4	8.1	21.1	7.9	0.7	3.5
250 - 499	27.5	13.2	36.8	12.2	11.1	35.1
500 - 749	22.7	22.8	22.8	15.7	15.6	17.5
750 - 999	16.3	16.9	7.0	12.2	17.0	12.3
1000 - 1499	10.8	17.6	10.5	16.9	18.5	19.3
1500 - 1999	3.6	8.8	1.8	9.8	11.9	5.3
2000 -	10.8	12.5	0.0	25.2	25.2	7.0
Total	100.0 (251)	100.0 (136)	100.0 (57)	100.0 (251)	100.0 (135)	100.0 (57)

Source: own survey 1985.

It is further interesting to look to the total householdincome, that may differentiate strongly dependent of the number of earners in the household. In figure 3.6 the share of the individual income to the total householdincome has been calculated.

The majority of the migrant households has only one income. More than 30% of the non-migrants and commuters participate for less than 40% in the total household income. The differences between the three groups can be explained by the different individual positions within the household. The migrants are mainly heads of household (75%) and are overrepresented in the older age categories. The main part of the commuters is less than 30 years old and, just like the non-migrants, consist for roughly 50% of persons who have a dependent position in the household (child).

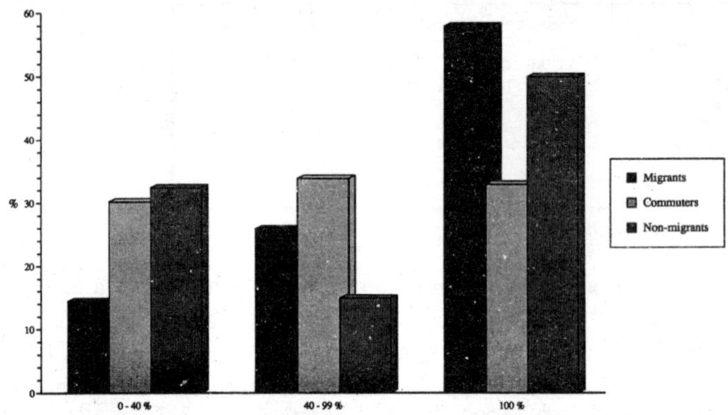

Figure 3.6 Share of individual income to total household income

3.5 Conclusions

The SIPCOT industries have created a demand for mainly skilled laborers, who were not available in Hosur. They were recruited from other areas, particularly the big cities in Tamil Nadu, resulting in migration to Hosur. The majority of the migrants are young men, often bachelors, making the age structure of Hosur unbalanced. Indirect migration effects of the growth of Hosur have been minor: the migration from the rural hinterland has not increased substantially. Some of the workers from the district have found a job in the Sipcot industries, though only on the lower paid levels.

It has been found that commuting is not an important phenomenon in the mobility structure of Hosur. Less than 10% of the employees at the industrial areas comes daily from outside. The commuters form a rather heterogeneous group. The richer workers among them give hardly any contribution to the development of Hosur because of their preference to reside in the metropole Bangalore. The poorer commuters come in particular from the small towns and not from the villages where the majority of the population lives. At the moment this group has no plans to go to Hosur, thus the rural areas do have some (minor) benefits from the economic activities in Hosur. But most of the commuters are young, dependent members of households and it is not impossible that in the near future, after a change in marital status their opinions may change.
Some groups in the working population of Hosur are underestimated in the present study. It is likely that poorer, unskilled casual laborers, descent from the surrounding villages, may also form an important part of the commuting process.

The demographic future of Hosur is not strong connected with the commuting patterns but more with the spatial behavior of the bachelors. If the last group stays in Hosur and forms families, the growth of Hosur will sustain for years: first in-migration of women, soon followed by many children. The need of facilities (e.g. educational) will rise and if they are provided, also the local population could benefit of it. If on the other hand the bachelors stay only a short time and leave, the industrial development will remain an enclave in the still backward district Dharmapuri.

4. Commuting and Migrant Adaptation

Eugene Bloemhard, Willem van Huijstee, Ab Kuiper, Hans van der Plicht

Internal migration, i.e. population mobility within a region, may have important socio-economic consequences for the region as a whole, the areas of origin and destination, and the (temporary) migrants themselves. One of the most important types of internal migration: the rural-to-urban form, is significant because of its close association with economic transformation from agriculture to non-agriculture and from a rural to an urban way of living.

In the fast growing body of literature on rural-urban migration it is usual to divide the different theoretical positions into two conflicting paradigms: the individual one and the structural one (Selier and Karim 1986). In the first approach it is assumed that rural to urban migration is the aggregate process of choice of individuals who are supposed to act like intervening variables such as age, position in the family, level of education, accessibility of information and transportation costs can be accommodated.

The second approach emphasizes the study of the structural conditions, determining the options and actions of individuals. Migration is the result of changes in the organization of production that affect the different classes unevenly. Rural-urban migration is not only a result of rational calculations, historical structural developments and cultural rules, but also of the existing social network of which the concerned household is a part. Friends, co-villagers and acquaintances both in the village and in the city can be important. Members of the social network can produce the necessary conditions for migration such as having information about the place of destination, money to travel and first assistance in town. The network, mostly wider than the household, is the social environment which influences the individual directly, filtering the macro-structural forces.

In this chapter attention will be paid to several aspects of the rural-urban migration process. In 4.1 an analysis has been made of the effects of commuting on both the individuals and the households they belong to. In the next two sections (4.2 and 4.3) a description will be given of how migrants adapt themselves with respect to housing and work. This has been illustrated with a case-study of the in-migration of poor rural migrants to the Ram Nagar area in Hosur. Finally, in 4.4 some conclusions will be drawn.

4.1 Commuting: the causes and effects

Both the regional development policy and the recent improvements in the transport system contributed to the rise of commuting to Hosur. The commuting process has effects on individuals and on the households they belong to. In the case of an individual, the increase of employment opportunities, the improved chance to get training in different kinds of jobs and the preservation of social ties, can be considered as positive effects. The journey to work and sometimes the 'forced' character of the job (i.e. sent by the head of the household) are possible negative effects.

On the level of the household, there are several positive effects: an increase of the total household-budget, spreading of risks, contacts made with new, differently structured labor markets, and possibly an opportunity for saving. These savings could be used for investment in means of production. A possible negative effect might be the influence of the urban environment that can lead to a different spending pattern.

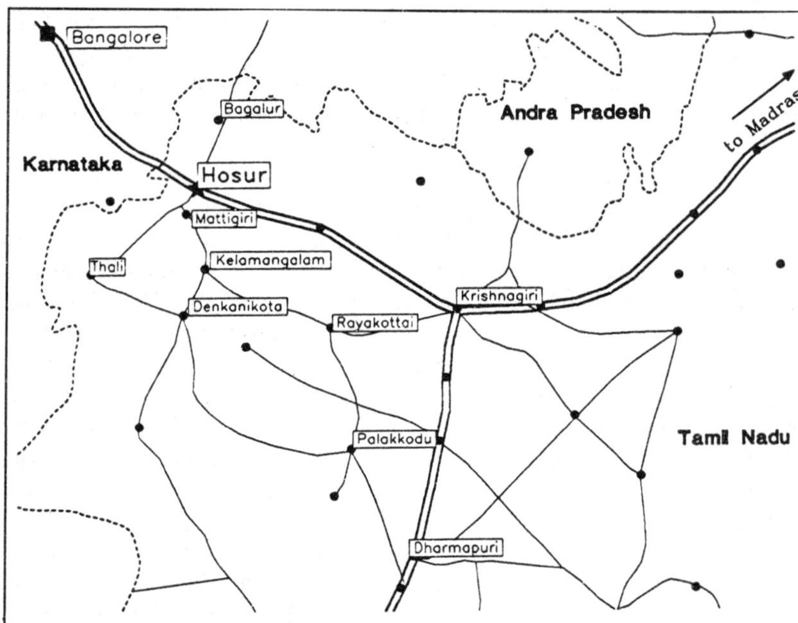

Map 3 The surroundings of Hosur

The research[1] concentrated on a limited number of small towns, which differed markedly from one another[2]. This selection was made to analyze the influence of the place of residence on the commuting process. The four places are: Mathigiri, Bagalur, Kelemangalam, Denkanikotta (see map 3). All these places are connected to Hosur by all-weather roads and public bus services.

4.1.1 The position of commuters in households and the labor market

Nearly half of all commuters are dependent children while 35.3% has the position of head of the household. Commuting has to be seen as an activity, which takes place in the interest of the total household. Only one third of the commuters said that they took the decision to work in Hosur on their own.
In table 4.1 one can find the labor structure and the relation with the economic activity of the commuters.

Table 4.1 Labor structure and economic activities of commuters in Hosur

	modern industries	manufact/ repair	shops	street	other activ.	total	total
Labor structure	abs	abs	abs	abs	abs	abs	%
Permanent high (>1000 Rs)	5	-	-	-	2	7	13.7
Permanent low (<1000 Rs)	15	-	-	-	1	16	31.4
Short-term	5	1	2	-	2	10	19.6
Casual	-	4	-	-	3	7	13.7
Dep.& Self-emp. (<1000 Rs)	-	1	1	5	-	7	13.7
Petit bourg. (>1000 Rs)	-	-	3	-	-	3	5.9
Other	-	-	-	-	1	1	2.0
Total abs(rel)	25(49.0)	6(11.8)	6(11.8)	5(9.8)	9(17.6)	51	(100.0)

Source: own survey 1986.

Thus the 'permanent' jobs are typically to be found in the modern industries (located at the industrial estates). 80% of the jobs created by companies situated at one of the estates are of the 'permanent' kind, against 11.5% of the jobs in town. These jobs are found in the category 'other', which is a highly heterogeneous group consisting mostly of service activities, including banks and governmental public services.

As can be expected a strong relationship between the position on the labor market and education has been established. The highest level of education has been found among permanent workers: 70%. In the subcategory of permanent workers earning more than Rs 1000 everyone has at least secondary school (SSLC). The less educated were found in the categories of the dependent and

[1] The results discussed in this paragraph originate from a stratified sample of 51 respondents from the commuter-survey data 1986 presented in chapter 3.

[2] These differences included distance to Hosur, number of inhabitants and existing livelihoods.

self-employed and casual workers. But even in the last category 14.3% had finished secondary school.

4.1.2 Household characteristics

The commuters from small towns belong to households who are in general larger than the migrant and non-migrant households living in Hosur. Among commuter households, an average size of 6.0 members was found, against 4.1 and 5.6 respectively for migrant and non-migrant households. The size ranges from 1 to 12 members with as largest category 4-6 members (53%).
Concerning the type of household (i.e. nuclear or extended), it can then be observed that the distribution over the various types hardly deviates from the distribution that is characteristic of the non-migrant households in Hosur, while it differs considerably from that of the households of migrants. The commuter households share with the original inhabitants of Hosur the traditional values: a rather large number of commuter households belongs to the category of extended families. The economic position of the commuter and non-migrant households differ completely.

Table 4.2 Total monthly income of commuter households compared with migrants and non-migrants in Hosur

income categories (Rs)	commuters	migrants	non-migrants
- 249	0.0	4.2	11.8
250 - 499	8.7	8.3	35.5
500 - 749	21.7	18.1	15.7
750 - 999	8.7	16.7	15.7
1000 - 1499	36.9	18.8	15.7
1500 - 1999	8.7	11.8	3.9
2000 and more	15.2	22.2	2.0
Total	100.0 (N=46)	100.0 (N=144)	100.0 (N=51)
average income	1298	1325	723
range from	350-4300		

Source: own survey 1986, Meijer and Heins 1987.

The average household income, as well as the distribution over the income categories of the commuter households, resemble the position taken by the migrant households more than that of the non-migrant households. However there are some differences. Within the migrant households the income is predominantly derived from the head of the household, while in the case of commuter households the income is frequently built up by contributions of several members. This is confirmed by the fact that couples with children older than 15 years have an average income of Rs 1728, while couples with younger children have an average income of Rs 1118.
In general one can say if more household members are present, the household income will increase, but at the same time the income of each individual member is decreasing. More important is the substantial contribution of the commuter in the total earnings of the household: on the average a 57.7%.

Thus, contrary to what is commonly stated, income from commuting forms a predominant part of the total household income. Loss of the commuters job severely jeopardizes the economic position of the household. With 17 of the jobs occupied by commuters in the categories of short-term and casual labor and therefore 'vulnerable' jobs (Harriss 1986), this means that one third of the households investigated lives in constant insecurity. However income out of wages is not the only variable that determines the economic position of the households. The accumulated wealth in terms of properties owned plays also an important role. The figures in this respect indicate that the economic position of the property-owning households is on average only marginally better, being for the most part households of small cultivators (see table 4.3 below).

Table 4.3 Owning of properties and the average income

	not owned		owned	
	income (Rs)	Number	income (Rs)	Number
land	1269	26	1405	17
live stock	1322	29	1357	13
means of production	1259	31	1354	10
house	1102	15	1393	31

Source: own survey 1986.

The economic position of the households is, of course, equally determined by the expenses these households have to meet. The figures in this respect reveal, that the large households which are found in the lower income categories live below the poverty line. The level of expenses in relation to the level of income determines the surpluses or deficits found in the household budgets. Some of the households may have the opportunity to save money, while others must incur debts. The figures show, that almost 30% of the households experience shortages in their current budgets. No wonder savings are much less common than debts (9 against 19 cases). Savings and debts can be seen as an indication of the future developments of the economic situation. Therefore an effort has been made to determine whether there have been any major changes in the economic position of the households investigated during the last 10 years. Eight respondents declared that they were worse off, against 31 respondents who said that they were better off. For this improvement of their economic situation the respondents frequently state as an explanation, that the number of household members with paid jobs has risen. No significant relation has been found between the total household income and existing savings or debts. Five of the households stated having savings declared that they had put money aside because of a forthcoming wedding (this is the reason most frequently given). These savings are held mostly in banking institutions (67%). There is little evidence that savings are used for the 'structural' improvement of the economic situation, for instance through investments. In 21 cases households had been forced to incur debts at one time or another. In 16 cases these debts were incurred with private persons, of whom 10 were professional money-lenders. The rates of interest that these money-lenders charge can be as high as 10% a month. Considering the incomes of these households, this means that they have to make great sacrifices to pay

the monthly rent and frequently are unable to pay installments.
The vulnerability of the economic position can be demonstrated with the example of the household of a tailor. Until recently, its economic situation was relatively good, because one of the daughters (the commuter) had found a good job at an electronic firm on the industrial estate. The income of the girl contributed more than 50% of the total household income. When she got married, the situation changed suddenly. She left the family that not only lost her income, but also had to incur debts for the dowry and the wedding.

4.1.3 Social and geographical background

The social system of Tamil Nadu is strongly determined by religion in general and caste in particular. The commuters can be divided into social strata according to religious background and caste. The relation of these groups with some other variables is shown in table 4.4. The largest differences are those between the household incomes of the Hindus belonging to the forward castes and the Christians[3]. The average income of the first group is more than three times the income of the last one. So the inequalities between population segments divided by religion or caste are large, though they are mediated through differences in educational level and thus in the position taken in the labor market. Most striking is the position taken by the backward castes with two third in permanent jobs (thus more than the average education might lead one to expect). This can only be explained as the result of the 'positive discrimination' policy of the government.
Information that has been gathered from panchayat officers reveals that Mathigiri is undoubtedly the most 'rural' place of residence in terms of the employment structure and the low level of amenities. Bagalur clearly has more and better employment opportunities because of the existence of three modern plants. The position taken by Denkanikotta in this respect is rather different. In this place there are remarkably few 'urban' jobs, while the relatively high level of amenities is caused by its status as a taluk headquarters.

How do these characteristics relate to the differences found in the commuting pattern? If Bagalur and Kelemangalam are left aside because of the small number of cases involved, and attention is concentrated on the comparison between Mathigiri and Denkanikotta, the following contrasts can be observed. The proportion of persons carrying out 'vulnerable' jobs in Denkanikotta is higher than in Mathigiri (40% against 32%) because the employment opportunities in the former are worse than in the latter. On the other hand the average educational level of the commuters from Denkanikotta is considerably higher (59.9% with SSLC or more against 34% in Mathigiri). So one can find relatively more people (20% versus 8%) from Denkanikotta in the better-paid

[3] This are often converted harijans.

permanent jobs (labor aristocracy) in Hosur. Still, 52% of the commuters from Mathigiri has found work in firms located on estates, against 46.7% of the people from Denkanikotta. This may be a reflection of the fact that commuting from Mathigiri is a complement of migration at an earlier date. People who had been able to find jobs in Hosur and wanted to settle there, had to live in Mathigiri instead. Through the tremendous increase in the demand for housing in Hosur, prices went up, making it financially impossible to settle in Hosur, especially for the poorer people.

Table 4.4 Education and income by caste and religion

	Forward caste	Backward caste	Muslim	Christian
educational level				
Below SSLC	10.0	55.6	85.7	100.0
SSLC or higher	90.0	44.5	14.3	0.0
Total	100.0	100.0	100.0	100.0
	(N=10)	(N=18)	(N=7)	(N=3)
type of job				
Permanent high (>1000 Rs)	10.0	22.2	0.0	0.0
Permanent low (<1000 Rs)	40.0	44.4	0.0	0.0
Short-term	30.0	11.1	14.3	66.7
Casual	0.0	11.1	57.1	33.3
Dep.& Self-emp. (<1000 Rs)	10.0	11.1	0.0	0.0
Petit bourg. (>1000 Rs)	10.0	0.0	28.6	0.0
Total	100.0	100.0	100.0	100.0
	(N=10)	(N=18)	(N=7)	(N=3)
total household income	1851	1141	1669	513
	(N=9)	(N=16)	(N=7)	(N=2)
contribution by commuter	715	627	671	358
	(N=10)	(N=18)	(N=7)	(N=3)

Source: own survey 1986.

Table 4.5 Average monthly household income and commuters contribution according to place of residence.

Place of residence	abs. income	N	contri-bution	N
Mathigiri	1284	24	691	25
Bagalur	1158	2	668	3
Kelemangalam	1362	7	622	7
Denkanikotta	1331	12	509	15
unknown	-	1	-	1
mean total sample	1298	46	621	51

Source: own survey 1986.

But, in spite of all these differences, table 4.5 shows that the household incomes of Denkanikotta and Mathigiri are nearly the same.

There is a considerable difference in the contribution made by the commuter to the total household income in respectively Denkanikotta and in Mathigiri (44.3% and 66.9%). A possible explanation may be the position of the commuter in the household. In the case of Denkanikotta, two third are children sent to work in Hosur. The commuter from Mathigiri is more often the head of the household and sole contributor to the household income. This is probably caused by the fact that these households have recently migrated to Mathigiri.

4.1.4 Future development

It is reasonable to assume that the quality of the job will influence the future behavior of the commuters. The degree of security inherent in a particular job may be a factor to the degree of job satisfaction. The level of satisfaction will once more affect the willingness to change jobs, or the wish to settle in Hosur. One quarter of the satisfied respondents and more than half of the less satisfied intended to change jobs. On the other hand, there is almost no difference between these groups in their willingness to settle in Hosur.

The tendency to move might be related to the age of the respondents, or, more likely, to their marital status. A considerable number of the commuters did not yet start their own families and will thus have ample opportunities for change. Especially after the birth of children, it becomes more and more difficult to move or change jobs. Furthermore, there are indications that the distance factor can affect the future behavior of commuters. Although the average willingness to settle in Hosur is already quite high (66.7%), it can be observed that this preparedness increases roughly with distance. But, only half of the respondents who stated that they were prepared to settle in Hosur have actual plans to move.

4.2 Migrant-adaptation in relation to housing

The success of finding a place to reside has a connection with the available information about the future place of living. Also the mobility of the migrant on the housing market is influenced by the sources of information. Paragraph 4.2.1 shows the influence of the sources of information and the migrants' adaptation to the housing market. The following two paragraphs deal with the housing situation and the satisfaction with the housing and environment. The last paragraph illustrates with a case-study the situation of poor in-migrants in the Ram Nagar area (see map 4).

4.2.1 Sources of information

Migrants who decided to leave their last place of residence are all in a unique situation. Some of them will have knowledge about their new place of residence while others lack this information at all. In both cases the adaptation processes in relation to housing may show differences.
Migrants without information will be less successful in finding good residence and will stay for a longer period at the place where they entered the housing market. This type of migrants with a limited spatial mobility may lack also any form of upward social mobility.
In the present research however, it was found that almost all migrants got in some way information about their new place of residence. The most important sources were the newspaper, friends, family and the employer. The nature of the

source of information can influence the success of the migrants' adaption to the housing market.

The data show that friends or family (informal contacts) play a very important role in finding residence for migrants. Migrants who didn't have the disposal of family or friends are not confronted with greater difficulties in finding residence, since these newcomers quite easily made contacts after arriving.

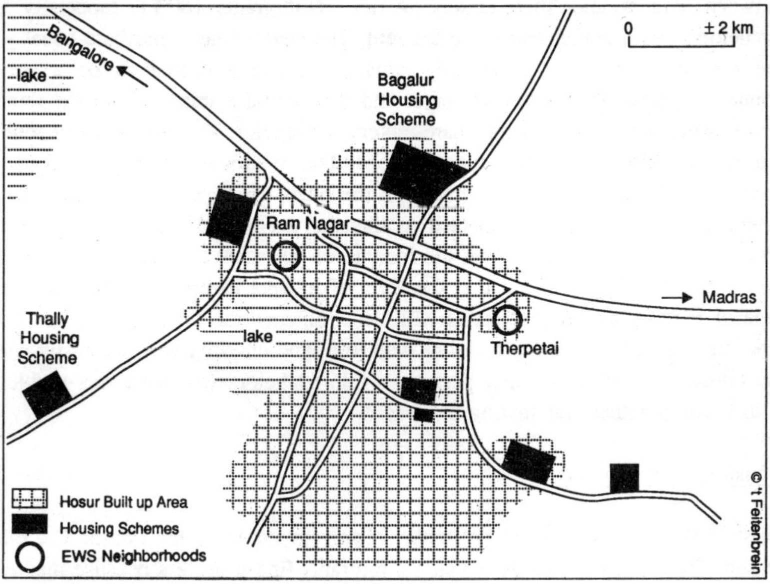

Map 4 Neighborhoods of Hosur

The same holds true for the transferred migrants. At the contrary to what one might expect, only 28% of them got support from the employer or government, while more than 60% of them were assisted by friends in finding residence.

A lot of migrants re-moved after a certain period (69%). There is a connection between re-moval and having or not having contacts (family/friends) before moving to Hosur. Those migrants who had friends in Hosur before they moved to this place, 52% of them re-moved. The migrants who didn't have family or friends in Hosur, re-moved in 85% of the cases.

4.2.2 The housing situation

The first form of shelter seems to function as temporary bridgehead. It can often be characterized as a 'living-together' situation. There is a connection between this form of residence and the presence of any relationship with people already living in Hosur prior to the arrival of the migrant. The migrants who had friends in Hosur before they moved to this place lived together with them in 75% of the cases. Those who had relatives before they moved to their new place lived together with them in only 39% of the cases, while 28% of this group lived together with friends. The 'living-together' situation of the migrants without any contacts before they moved, is more diversified. 54% of them is living together with (new) friends and a considerable part of this group is living on his own.

The majority of the migrants live in rented houses. A distinction can be made between renters and share-renters. A lot of migrants (60%), especially the bachelors, live together and share the rent. The share-renter contribute equally to the rent contrary to a subtenancy situation. There appeared to be a strong connection between the type of renter and the marital status: 82% of the renters was married while 90% of the share-renters is bachelor. The two types of renters are also working in different types of jobs. The renters are mainly found in the 'professional jobs'. The share-renters on the other hand are found mainly in the category 'skilled labor'. Connected to this the average monthly income of the renters is higher (Rs 1542) than the income of the share-renters (Rs 982). From this it can not be concluded that the level of income completely determines the type of renting, the marital status will also influence the type of renting. Those who are married and living together with wife and children will not easily share the house or room with other persons, while bachelors will have less problems with living together and sharing the rent.

Housing improvements

Most of the respondents did not make improvements upon the house. The main reason (56%) not to improve is that the migrants find it useless because they rent the house. In comparison with the other areas of Hosur a relatively high percentage (79%) of the 'not-improvers' can be found in the Bagalore housing scheme. A possible explanation is that in this area the facilities are much better than in the other parts of Hosur. Less than one third of the respondents have made improvements. The kind of improvements differs between the type of area. In the Bagalore housing scheme they exist mainly of fitting better locks on the doors and making more water taps. In the other schemes much of the money on improvements is spend on fencing the house/garden. The improvements in south-east, south-west Hosur and Therpetai are of a more elementary type. Here, much of the money on improvements is spend on repairing the roof (leakages). In south and north-east Hosur most of the improvements exist of (re)painting inside and outside the house.

4.2.3 Satisfaction with the housing and environment

So far we paid attention to the question how and in which way migrants adapt themselves as far as housing is concerned. Now, the discussion will focus on the success of the above described adaptation-strategy and on the question whether the migrants are satisfied with their current residence.

The three most important housing facilities are water, electricity and sanitary facilities. In general we find that these basic facilities are very common in most houses, especially in the Bagalore housing scheme and the other recently built schemes. In the other areas 60% of the respondents is not satisfied about the toilet- and waterfacilities. Only 26% is not satisfied with the facilities on electricity. But in general the absence of electricity is not interpreted as a big problem. In table 4.6 the level of satisfaction of the households with and without plans for moving is presented. It is remarkable that a majority of the 'very satisfied' migrants have plans for moving. The lack of financial possibilities may be a reason for the less satisfied households not having plans to move.

Table 4.6 Level of satisfaction and plans for house-moving

	Plans for moving		No plans for moving	
	Abs.	Rel.	Abs.	Rel.
Very satisfied	50	74.6	17	25.4
Moderate satisfied	5	50.0	5	50.0
Not satisfied	2	22.2	7	77.8
Total	57	66.3	29	33.7

Source: own survey 1985.

Problems with the landlord is a reason to move for those respondents who are very satisfied with their house. The moderate satisfied respondents are willing to move, because the house is too small in their opinion. The unsatisfied respondents want to change their housing because the facilities inside and around the house are insufficient.

For some respondents the environmental facilities are very important. In general they are not satisfied at all about the facilities in their housing estates. Especially in Bagalore housing scheme schools, shops and sportfacilities are mentioned to be insufficient. In the other areas of Hosur, the level of satisfaction on these facilities is much lower. In Therpetai and south Hosur the absence of shops and good bus connections as well as bad roads has been stated as major problems. A fundamental problem in all estates is the refuse collection. But in contrast with the other areas the respondents in the Bagalore housing scheme are very unsatisfied with this facility. The number of garbage-baskets is insufficient and the cleaning up of them is very irregular.

4.2.4 Ram Nagar: the housing of poor in-migrants in Hosur

This paragraph contains the results of a study to the poor in-migrants and their housing situation in Ram Nagar, a slum area close to the old center of Hosur. Attention will be paid to the reasons why the in-migrants settle down in Ram Nagar, the physical infrastructure and the socio-economic aspects of the neighborhood.

Reasons to come to Ram Nagar

The average monthly household income of the poor in-migrants is Rs 450. About two third of these group has come from the countryside. More than 80% originates from the Dharmapuri District or Karnataka within a distance of 75 kilometers from Hosur. Almost one quarter lived in nearby cities or towns, like Bangalore, Dharmapuri and Krishnagiri. 15% of the respondents mentioned Madras, Delhi and other far away urban areas, while 10% left distant rural areas before they came to Hosur. As can be expected, the main reason to come to Hosur was an economic one. The choice for Ram Nagar within Hosur depended on several reasons; the most important were:

- low rent or price of dwelling (30%)
- availability of (better) dwelling or plot (23%)
- proximity to location of the job (13%)
- presence of family or friends (9%).

Physical infrastructure

Ram Nagar is situated within a triangle of main roads connecting Hosur with Bangalore, Madras and the southern part of the Dharmapuri district. The site consists of two ground levels: a lower part formed by an approximately five meters deep dry moat and a higher 'fort-hill' part. The surface of the moat is a mixture of true laterite and bog soils. Parts of the soil material, often in combination with rocks and other kinds of materials, is often used to build brick and mud-wall houses in Ram Nagar. On the hill site for instance there is a brick factory.

The roads around Ram Nagar are all asphalted and relatively well maintained, while within the area itself none of the streets has been hardened.
On the north and western brim of the fort-hill and the eastern dike we come across levelled streets, which are badly drained by unfinished and poorly maintained canals. The street and parcel pattern of Ram Nagar is highly determined by the natural site factors. The absence of a well functioning drainage system caused serious hydrological problems. In the moat area there is no such a system at all, but unlike the situation on the higher hill-area the natural drainage in the moat is bad. The water-table frequently rises and the soil moisture then produces a too high percentage of moisture within many houses. In general however the level of this artificial drainage system does not deviate very much from the rest of Hosur, except for the planned housing schemes. The north-east side of the area has been build most densely with also some multi-storied buildings. All of these buildings are in general of relatively good quality. A limited number of inferior houses consist of mud walls and a roof made of palm leaves. Most of the houses have consolidated mud walls and a tiled roof. A smaller part has walls of dried or semi-burned bricks. Only a few houses are composed of concrete or burned bricks. These last ones are concentrated around the commercial center of Ram Nagar. The infamous shacks erected of garbage

are almost completely absent in the area. The few ones which we do find here, form a temporary home of some migrants (mostly construction laborers).

At night Ram Nagar is scarcely lit by approximately 40 lampposts, most of them are situated along the streets on the hill-area and the eastern dikes. The total public water-supply system is equipped with one communal well, two bore wells (pumps) and five water taps. These last ones have been connected with the public water works of Hosur. They deliver potable water to the households in Ram Nagar for some hours a day in the wet season. This means that the dwellers depend on three public water-supply facilities for the rest of the day. Besides, the system often malfunctions and this brings along severe problems of water shortage especially in the dry seasons.

The absence of communal latrines as well as private latrines in almost all dwellings does not only cause great inconvenience for the dwellers but it also increases the chance of diseases. The level of facilities in comparison with the rest of Hosur is low, but the quality of the buildings is improving. Finally there are in Hosur areas which are worse off, for instance Therpetai.

The majority of the EWS in-migrants in Ram Nagar lives in a dwelling smaller than 16 m^2. One third ownes the house they live in. The prices of the houses range upto Rs 10,000. The average EWS renter pays Rs 57 a month, this is 15% to 30% of the income. The facilities are very poor: only 30% uses electricity and there are hardly private latrines, none of the dwelling has its own water tap. This point has the highest priority for the inhabitants as far as improvements are concerned. Infrastructural improvements and educational facilities have a low priority.

<u>Socio-economic characteristics</u>

The residential part of Ram Nagar is populated by 5000 to 6000 inhabitants. Population density amounts to 250 people per acre; the agricultural area is nearly uninhabited. More than fifty per cent of the households consists of younger families. The average family size is between 3 and 4 members. The greater part of the dwellers have lived in Hosur for more than five years. In Ram Nagar there are a few small industrial activities, like a brick factory and candy manufacture. Other economic activities are: the home production of beedies and incense sticks; handicrafts like sculpture making, mat-weaving, tailoring, butchering, forging and welding, car repairing; commercial activities or merchandising (especially selling of food stuffs); and some agricultural activities like cattle breeding. The most common characteristics of these activities are their casualness and informality. The impact of these activities on the income situation of the households of migrants is small because most of the economic population works outside Ram Nagar.

4.3 Migrant adaptation in relation to work

The growth pole policy in Hosur has resulted in the creation of new work and the arrival of many migrants. In this section attention will be paid to the question how migrants adapt themselves in Hosur as far as work is concerned. The main theme in 4.3.1 is to what extent and from whom the migrants have got information about the job opportunities in Hosur. In the next paragraph we will analyze the job opportunities of the migrants on the Hosur labor market. Further a short description will be given of the role of remittances and savings (4.3.3) and finally we will discuss the migrants' judgement of their labor position.[4]

4.3.1 Sources of information

The migrants did not come to Hosur without preparation. Before their departure all migrants have made inquiries about the job opportunities in this town (see table 4.7). This information comes from different sources; the most important ones are relatives, friends (who are both mostly resident in Hosur) and the newspapers. This last source of information has been important especially for migrants, who were already employed in their last place of residence. Next to it, also the government and the employers appear to be important sources of information; 18 migrants (19,8%) have been transferred to Hosur by their employer (government or private company).

Table 4.7 Labor background of the migrants by sources of information

Sources of information	Labor background			
	employed	unemployed	student	total
relatives	13,1	66,7	25,9	18,6
friends	11,5	--	22,2	14,3
newspapers	24,6	--	11,1	19,8
government	3,3	--	3,7	3,3
government-transfer	13,1	--	--	8,8
employer	4,9	33,3	25,9	12,1
employer-transfer	16,4	--	--	11,0
self	9,8	--	7,5	8,8
other	3,3	--	3,7	3,3
TOTAL	100,0 (61)	100,0 (3)	100,0 (27)	100,0 (91)

Source: own survey 1985.

For the students, besides relatives and friends, also employers have been important sources of information. Some employers in Hosur have visited schools and training institutes in the surroundings of Hosur in order to select the best

[4] For this research a sample has been drawn of the migrants in Hosur. The sample consists of 91 male migrants, who are in general well educated; a large majority possesses at least the SSLC-certificate. As far as the labor background in their last place of residence is concerned, 61 migrants (67%) were working, 27 migrants (30%) were studying, where as three migrants were unemployed then.

students for their company. These students were offered a job in Hosur, mainly as a skilled laborer. Almost 90% of the migrants had on arrival in Hosur no problem to find a job. Besides the transferred migrants (20%), most of the other migrants had arranged a job before they moved to this town. The migrants who had no job when they arrived in Hosur, succeeded in finding work within one month.

It can be concluded, that nearly all migrants who were unemployed or studying in their last place of residence, succeeded very quickly in finding work in Hosur. This applies also to the migrants with a job in their last place of residence. In table 4.8 one can find to what extent the income of these migrants has increased after their migration to Hosur.

Table 4.8 Change in monthly income in Rs after migration to Hosur

	increase in income	decline in income
1 - 500	39.3%	8.2%
500 - 1000	26.2%	4.9%
1000 and more	11.5%	3.3%
No income change	6.6%	
Average income change	Rs 565	Rs 652
(total number of migrants: 61)		

Source: own survey 1985.

Most migrants (47; 77%) have now a higher wage than in their last place of residence; a great majority earns now up to Rs 1000 per month more than in their last place of residence. Particularly the migrants who are working for private companies and the self-employed migrants have now higher wages than before. On the other hand it is striking that at present nearly all migrants who have been transferred to Hosur by the government, do not earn more than in their last place of residence.

4.3.2 The labor position of the migrants

The SIPCOT-Industries have created a demand for mainly skilled laborers, who were not available in Hosur. It is therefore not astonishing that 76% of the migrants has found a job in the companies at the three industrial estates. The others are working in Hosur-town, where they are employed mainly by government institutions and banks. Most self-employed migrants (8) started their company or shop in Hosur-town (for example a construction company, a metal trade and a milkman). There appears to be a important difference in income between the migrants working in Hosur-town and at the industrial estates.

In table 4.9 it appears that 63% of the migrants working in Hosur-town, earns more than Rs 1000 per month, where as 69% of the migrants with a job in the SIPCOT-Industries has an income of less than Rs 1000. Both labor groups are in the two distinguished areas different represented. So belongs 76% of the migrants who are employed at the industrial estates, to the labor category 'permanent wage workers low' (< Rs 1000 per month). In Hosur-town it is just the other way round; there the migrants belong mainly to the richer labor groups, such as 'permanent wage workers high' (>= Rs 1000) and the 'petit-bourgeois' (self-employed workers with a monthly income of more than Rs 1000).

Table 4.9 Place of work by monthly income in Rs

monthly income (Rs)	industrial estates	Hosur-town
- 499	20.6	13.6
500 - 999	48.5	22.7
1000 - 1499	8.8	45.5
1500 and more	22.1	18.2
TOTAL	100.0 (68)	100.0 (22)

Source: own survey 1985.

The migrants who belong to this last category, have the highest average income of all labor groups, namely Rs 3250 per month. The fact that a majority of the migrants who are working in the Sipcot industries, earns less than Rs 1000 per month, is not only caused by the overrepresentation of the poorer permanent wage workers. It is also explained by the fact, that many richer permanent wage workers of the SIPCOT industries do not reside in Hosur, but commute every day to their work, especially from Bangalore.
Between the two distinguished areas there are not only differences in income but equally in age, marital status and job-arrangement. Hosur-town is mainly characterized by married migrants, who are mainly older than 30 years. Almost all of these migrants are richer permanent wage workers or self-employed workers. (See table 4.10).

In Hosur-town more than 45% of the migrants (mostly richer permanent wage workers) has been transferred, mainly by the government. At the industrial estates the picture is completely different; this area is mainly characterized by young, unmarried migrants, who had their job arranged before they moved to Hosur. They belong almost completely to the category 'permanent wage workers low'. As one can conclude from table 4.11, the transferred migrants have in general the highest wages; 61% has a monthly income of at least Rs 1500. The income position of the migrants who were not transferred to Hosur is obviously inferior. A majority of the migrants with a job-arrangement has a monthly income of less than Rs 1000, whilst 50% of the migrants without a job-arrangement earns less than Rs 500 per month. So besides a short period of unemployment after their migration to Hosur, these migrants have also the greatest chance of a low income. A majority of these migrants belongs to the category 'permanent wage workers low'.

It was expected that the migrants who had no job-security on arrival in Hosur, would change work relatively more often than the migrants with a job-arrangement. The reason for this expectation was, that these migrants are forced to take any job on arrival in Hosur in order to make their living. But there appears to be no difference between these two groups as far as change of work is concerned. Only eight migrants (9%) changed work once in Hosur; it concerned young casual wage workers and poorer permanent wage workers.

Table 4.10 Place of work by age, marital status and job-arrangement

	industrial estates (%)	Hosur-town (%)
≤ 30 years	79.4	36.4
> 30 years	20.6	63.6
single	69.1	27.3
married	30.9	72.7
job arranged	76.5	50.0
transfer	11.8	45.5
no job arranged	11.8	4.5

Source: own survey 1985.

More than half of the migrants who changed work in Hosur (63%), have got a training on-the-job in this town as against 24% of the migrants, who have still their first job. In spite of the high educational level, still 25 migrants (28%) have got a training on-the-job in Hosur, especially a technical training. Mainly young migrants with lower skilled jobs ('permanent wage workers low') have got a training.

Table 4.11 Job-arrangement by monthly income in Rs

income (Rs)	job arranged	transfer	no job arranged
- 499	14.3%	5.6%	50.0%
500 - 999	41.3%	11.1%	20.0%
1000 - 1499	20.6%	22.2%	30.0%
1500 and more	23.8%	61.1%	0.0%
Total	100.0% (63)	100.0% (18)	100.0% (10)

Source: Own survey 1985.

4.3.3 Remittances and savings

In spite of their migration to Hosur, the family-ties are still strong. Nearly all migrants (95%) have visited their relatives a couple of days during the past six months. Next to it also many migrants (53%) remit money to their relatives every month (on an average Rs 397 per month). But the amount of remittances varies with the income; most migrants with a monthly income of less than Rs 1000 are not able to send home more than Rs 250 per month, where as the majority of the richer migrants (>= Rs 1000 per month) is able to remit at least Rs 250 per month. The majority of the migrants who transfer money, consists of bachelors. Because the bachelors are mainly living together with other bachelors - resulting in lower costs of residence - they can more easily put away a part of their income for their relatives than married migrants. For the majority of the unmarried migrants who earns less than Rs 1000 per month, remittances are more important than savings. First they remit a certain amount of money to their relatives; if there is still any money left, than they save this. 46% of the migrants is able to save every month. Married migrants appear to save relatively more often than bachelors because they remit less money to relatives elsewhere. Besides, they have in general higher wages than bachelors; 46% of them earns more than Rs 1500 per month. The migrants save mostly for good education for their children, for an own house, for their own company/shop or for their own marriage. On an average the migrants save Rs 413 per month, but also in this case the amount of savings varies with the income. The migrants with a monthly income of up to Rs 500, are not able to save at all.

4.3.4 The migrants' judgement of their labor position

One can say that in general the migrants are satisfied with their present position in Hosur. 79% of the migrants is satisfied with the number of working hours. Most migrants work eight hours a day and six days a week. But the longer they work, the more they are discontented; this applies especially to the following labor groups: 'permanent wage workers high', 'dependent and self-employed workers' and the 'petit-bourgeois'. Some of them work more than ten hours a day and sometimes even seven days a week.
Only 56% of the migrants is satisfied with their income; particularly the migrants with a monthly income of less than Rs 1000, such as the 'permanent wage workers low', the 'dependent and self-employed workers' and the 'casual wage workers', are discontented with their income. On the other hand, 89% of the migrants with a monthly income of at least Rs 1500, such as the 'permanent wage workers high' and the 'petit-bourgeois', is satisfied with their income.

The security of work appears to be high; 92% is not afraid of losing their job. None of the migrants who are employed by government institutions, is afraid of being dismissed. The main reasons for the fact that many migrants are not afraid of losing their job, are that they have a permanent contract of employment (45%) and that they have a good relation with their management (22%). Next to it, nearly all self-employed migrants foresee a prosperous future for their company or shop in Hosur. In spite of the high security of work, still one-third of the migrants is looking for another job. There appears to be a relation between the search for another job and the income: 76% of the migrants who are looking for another job, earns not more than Rs 1000 per month. Especially young, unmarried skilled laborers at the industrial estates want to change work. Besides the discontent with their income, some migrants are looking for another job, because they want to work in another place than Hosur. Most of them want to go back to their last place of residence, which is in all cases a city. They want to leave Hosur not only because of family circumstances, but also because of the shortage of facilities in Hosur, such as shops, education- and recreation facilities.

4.4 Conclusions

When looking upon the effects of variables that belong to the setting of the commuting process, the following information has been obtained. First, it has been found that the impact of the social system on the total household income is the most pronounced result. The data with relation to the places of residence show that the largest differences exist between Mathigiri and Denkanikotta. One particularly important difference was the level of the commuter's contribution to the household income, that of the commuters from Mathigiri being considerably larger. This is probably due to the type of household involved and the position the commuter occupies in the households.
Regarding the changes over longer periods of time no conclusive evidence has been found. The future behavior of the respondents is expected to depend upon the distance factor: the people that live in Denkanikotta, thus further removed from their work spot, are sooner prepared to settle in Hosur than the others. Given the large number of respondents who are prepared to settle in Hosur, a growth may be expected well above the average growth rate of cities belonging to this size category. Thus, in spite of recent housing schemes, the pressure on the housing market will probably temporarily remain. And so neighboring small villages may witness an influx of migrants too.

In relation to the individual it has been found that a large proportion of the jobs are insecure and the better part of the labor market suffers from a relatively restricted ease of entry. Turning to the households the following has been discovered. The income derived from commuting is necessary to cope with the expenses that have to be met daily, so almost nothing remains for other purposes. In many cases the economic future of the commuter households in highly insecure, because of the fact that the job the commuter occupies is insecure, while his contribution to the household income is important, if not vital. Those households that for their income rely entirely on the commuters income could well be more vulnerable then ever. The data showed that the households that owned any properties were only slightly better off.

Nearly all migrants who were unemployed or studying in their last place of residence, succeeded very quickly in finding work in Hosur. This also applies to the migrants with a job in their last place of residence. Before their departure all migrants have made inquiries about the job opportunities in Hosur. The most important sources of information are relatives, friends and newspapers. Migrants who did not have the disposal of family or friends are not confronted with greater difficulties in finding residence, since these newcomers quite easily made contacts after arriving.

The majority of the migrants live in rented houses. A subdivision can be made between renters and share-renters. The renters who are mainly found in the 'professional jobs', are often married and will not easily share the house or room with other persons. Bachelors, mostly skilled laborers, will have less problems with living together and sharing the rent. Most of the poor in-migrants who did come to Ram Nagar, selected this area because of the low rents and the availability of (better) dwellings or plots. In spite of the migration to Hosur, the family ties are still strong. More than half of the migrants remit money to their relatives every month. In particular bachelors, who have low costs of residence, can easily put away a considerable part of their income for their relatives.

In general the migrants are satisfied with their present position in Hosur. The security of work appears to be high, but especially young, unmarried skilled laborers at the industrial estates want to change work. It is remarkable that a majority of the very satisfied migrants have plans for house-moving. Very often this group has problems with the landlords. Finally one can conclude that the majority of the migrants were very unsatisfied about the environmental facilities in their residential area.

5. WOMEN AT THE LABOR MARKETS OF HOSUR

Joanne Heyink Leestemaker

In the present context of South India women play another role in life than men. This sexe-specific distinction is hardly found in the general literature of growth pole policy, migration, urbanization and modernization. Effects of growth pole policy on women is not considered by academics as special issue to study. Neither it is seen as an important topic in the phase of preparing policies, nor in the phase of policy evaluations. Usually it is taken for granted that 'economic growth' reaches women automatically by creating men's employment. This 'trickling-down' effect through the sexes may be even more deficient as through social classes.

A study about the role of women in the labor market in a growth pole should start with a set of assumptions. In this research[1] the following assumptions have been made:

- Innovations are not taken place for each individual under the same conditions, with the same timing, along the same path and with the same price.
- In the given framework of age, caste/class, sexe, race and migration background every individual makes his or her own biography within the social processes that take place.
- In the current South-Indian context women perform another function in life than men.

Women's daily life is largely determined by their marital status, number of children and composition of the household. The poorest women are economically pressed to work for money to contribute to the household income.

This chapter has been divided into two sections. In the first part we look at life in Hosur from the point of view of work. Using a theoretical model the principle of diverse labor markets in Hosur in 1986 will be described. Then this model is filled in with specific forms of employment for women (5.1). For the description of paid (5.1.1) and unpaid work (5.1.2) of women in different phases of the life cycle a selection from different segments of the labor markets has been made (5.1.3).

The second part takes the viewpoint of life expectations of individual women. We analyze the ways women can act at the labor markets (5.2.1), do they have access to better paid and less tiring jobs? The static model is reconstructed to the

[1] As research unit the individual woman is chosen, not the entire household (N=50). Because a stratified sample is drawn, the generalizations that can be made to the total female population of Hosur will be limited.

more flexible 'labor mountains' (5.2.2). Within all kind of constraints women can choose their own life path on these 'mountains'. Mobility and freedom of choice are restricted in several ways. Especially women with a rural migration background, without formal education, capital or credit facilities and without a network of contacts, do have less freedom or mobility at the labor market of Hosur.

The logic of their daily life, which contains a combination of paid, money saving and unpaid work, is made visible with the time-use method. This is illustrated with the daily paths of some women (5.2.3). Finally some conclusions are drawn in 5.3.

5.1 Labor markets of Hosur

We will start with an overview of categories of work - paid and unpaid - done by women. The combination of occupations, labor relations, payment and status of work is placed in a labor market model (figure 5.1), characterizing the multi-structural transition stage to a monetary industrial society[2]. It composes of different markets: the formal (official organized labor, large-scale capitalist mode of production), the informal (unofficial organized labor, small-scale mode of production) and the shadow labor market, where no money is transferred for production.

Because of the sexe-segregation at the labor markets the place of women's work is always at the bottom of each segment. This implies for each segment the lowest paid work, with lowest status. The best paid and valued segments of the labor market - as skilled staff at the formal market and initiators at the informal market - are male dominated. (Illich 1982; Reich, Gordon & Edwards 1980). Female initiators at the informal labor market need the context of the family. They only can do the job under the public umbrella of a male family member, preferably the husband, father or brother.

Between the formal and informal market there is a growing special market, where work, under cheap conditions of the informal sector, is done for the formal labor market. The system of subcontracting also takes place in this special section of the labor market[3]. The shadow labor market deals with work outside the monetary sector. Ivan Illich, who coined the term, uses 'shadow labor' to describe the historical development process of colonialism and capitalism. Since the introduction of the monetary system in every society, a variable part of total labor can be qualified as 'shadow labor'. Which part of communal labor precisely is unpaid depends upon political and economical decisions. At the level of the individual household, economic wealth and the

[2] Kalpagam describes the labor structure in India as: "Industrialization had thus been taking place in this country under conditions of a multi-structural economy, where lower structures are still significant in terms of the employed labor force despite the fact that industrialization and general economic development have succeeded in transforming these lower structures and adapting them to meet the requirements of capitalist development." (1984; p. 199).

[3] In chapter 2 on industrial policy and the role of small-scale industries, another structuring of labor markets has been used.

prevailing ideology play an important role. The division of unpaid work between the sexes however is pretty fixed: as long as women are part of the household, men will not do unpaid work in the household. Taking care of drinking water, laundry and food are in the first instance women's tasks. Men take on 'management tasks', like dealing with post-office and government agencies.

Formal labor market in three segments

1. specialized skilled staff in modern industry	2. supporting staff members + permanent wage laborers
[capital-intensive sectors]	
3. uncertain wage laborers with low status and payment without career prospects [capital-extensive sectors]	

Informal labor serving the formal labor market

subcontracting, overtime, contract labor [labor-intensive sectors]

Independent informal labor market in three segments

1. private initiators with network of contacts irregular earnings	2. employed by private initiators piece-wage/daily wage
[with possibility to invest]	
3. casual labor own working power as only source of income [without possibility to invest]	

Shadow labor market in three segments

1. self subsistence own support	2. subsistence of others support of others
[without transfer of money]	
3. complete subsistence [outside the monetary system]	

Figure 5.1 Labor market of Hosur, according to Illich and Reich, Gordon & Edwards

The first segments of the distinguished labor markets give (relative) the most security, the third segments give the less.

Women's formal labor market in three segments

1. doctor, schoolmistress, personnel manager	2. telegrapher, clerk, stenographer, (data-)typist supervisor, teacher, nurse
3. industrial worker, trainee, daily worker on silk farm sweeper	

Informal labor serving the formal labor market

agarbatti-homeworker (incense), gummer of bags, beedi-homeworker, flower-stringer; structural overtime in factories

Independent informal labor market in three segments

1. milk woman, dohbi shopkeeper tailor, sari-sari shopkeeper middlewoman in rubbish and old iron producer/seller dried dung /firewood/kerosine/hay small vendors of vegetable	2. dohbi, trainee in shops servant, water carrier fast-food producers, coolie on the building site spinner / dyer of silk gummer of bags, flower stringer
3. coolie on the building site or the stone-factory, dohbi, rag-picker, beggar, priest, prostitute	

Shadow labor market in three segments

1. to carry water, washing, food production, cooking, cleaning for one's own	2. to carry water, washing, food production, cooking, cleaning for family
3. to build an own house, draw-well to cultivate own food/fuel	

Figure 5.2 Labor market model (based on figure 5.1), for women's work in Hosur[4].

5.1.1 Paid women's work in Hosur

The labor market model is used as structure for presentation of the research results. Besides income and average number of working hours per day, position in the labor spectrum gives an indication for the (un)security of employment. Eighty per cent of the respondents are working for money.

Formal labor market

Sexe- and class-segregation at labor markets are important for the classification of jobs and their status and payment (Bergmann 1980). In Hosur consequences of this mechanism meant that no women can break through to the best section of

[4] Sari-sarishops (literally: many small things) are run in wooden boxes at eye level along the road. The box can be closed with a hatch. Many Asian cities are full of these shops, run by women, with female customers.

the labor market. In the second best section (supporting staff members and permanent wage laborers) are 'typical' women's jobs as typist, stenographer, teacher or nurse. In fruit-canning and electronic factories there are female supervisors, heading work units of six to ten female laborers.
The majority of these women are unmarried (76%) and have a medium education level with some years of work experience. Three quarter of the women has a permanent job, while the other women work on a temporary contract base (mostly one year). The wage level depends for an important part on the size of the company. Big enterprises with locations all over India pay better salaries than local businesses. For example, a supervisor of Elcot (state oriented) monthly earns Rs 350 (1986 prices), and her colleague of English Electric (national oriented) receives Rs 850, while she is two years younger and lower skilled.

At the bottom of the formal labor market we find laborers of the few factories which recruit female employees, and coolies of the governmental silk plantation. Most work is done low paid on contract base in labor-intensive sectors. Some enterprises in the industrial area have adopted the 'trainee-system': most of the normal labor force works as 'trainee' for some period. Tropican, a fruit-canning company, contracts - except the staff - only 'trainees' as employees. STEP, a company in electronics, has nearly half of the female workers on trainee-contract. They earn Rs 150 per month, doing the same unskilled job on the assembly line as permanent workers, who earn the double amount. For companies using this system the low cost of labor is an advantage, the run-over of employees can be a disadvantage, but as long as many women are looking for work, this disadvantage is nihil.

Informal labor market

The informal labor market - more than the formal - knows a great variety of occupations practiced by women. Within occupation groups there is a sexual division of labor in payment and status. For instance, within the group of water carriers there is a strict sexual division of labor: female water carriers serve private households by carrying drinking water in pots on head or shoulder from the source to the house. Male carriers serve large consumers as restaurants and lodges, transporting the water on bullock cart, barrow or bicycle.

A clear occupation-bounded sexual division is found in some subcontracting relations between formal and informal labor market. The subcontracting employers are looking for cheapest labor; in most cases this is found in home-based female workers. Agarbatti sticks (incense) are made by women, because they are the only ones willing to produce thousand sticks for Rs 1.5. Often this is the only way for mothers with small children and without money or skill to survive.
One can find in the same category beedi-working, food preparation and flower tieing; it asks for accuracy and quickness and it hardly pays. Moreover the work is easy to do, no machinery is needed and no investments have to be made. (Banerjee 1985; Bhatty 1984).

The first segment of the informal labor market contains private initiators with the possibility to invest. These people start to trade on their own risk or to produce and sell their own product. Women belonging to this segment, are married and work together with their husbands and - sometimes - children. 40% of them are unskilled, while 60% has some years of formal education. The women are spending an average of 9.5 hours per day on paid employment (family labor). The (family) income in this segment is running up from Rs 200 to 1000 Rs per month. This income is often unpredictable because of lack of contract. Furthermore all kinds of production costs (and often debts) are to be paid first. The second segment is characterized by relations of subcontracting, in the same way as the grey zone between formal and informal labor: 'dependent labor' (20%) and 'hidden wage labor' (80%) in Bromley's labor spectrum (Bromley 1985). These women are working for other households in a permanent labor relation without a formal contract (fetching water, servants) and women working on piece-rate base (agarbatti, beedies, food, flower-tieing, gumming of bags).

The level of formal education is low: 80% unskilled, and the rest has some years of formal education. Four out of five belong to the scheduled caste. The women are spending an average of 9 hours per day on paid labor and their income is running up from Rs 120 to 360 per month. Because of non-official contracts their income is mostly more stable than in the first segment of the informal labor market but at the same time much lower, with less possibilities for improvement. Debts are dominating their lives equally. These debts are mostly caused by a disaster in their vulnerable livelihood: illness, death, robbery, fire; the abuse of alcohol is another cause. Debts are often causing more debts because of high interest asked by money lenders.

The relation between formal and informal labor markets is clear: the water carriers and servants are working for households which can permit themselves to subcontract this kind of labor. One or more members of these more prosperous households are working on the formal labor market or belong to the successful self-employed. In this segment the work is also done within the context of the family. Not necessarily organized by a male member, like in the first segment, but done merely together with children, who are enlarging the earnings by their cooperation. Within the context of family work men often play the role of middleman between home-based workers and the subcontractor[5]. Dohbis and servants are often poor female heads of households, living without an earning husband.

The lowest segment of the informal labor market contains female casual workers, without formal labor contract. They have their own labor power as only source of income. These women are looking for construction work every day again, or feeding themselves through marginal trade. The end of the day is the same as the beginning: earned money is immediately converted into daily food.

[5] In her research of home-based lace makers of Narsapur Maria Mies describes the dynamic of the sexual division of labor. Husbands of the homeworkers are applying as middlemen, because of the lack of employment for themselves.

School is never attended by 87% of the respondents in this group. Half of the women are living with a husband; all have children. The cash income runs up from Rs 90 to 170 per month, for an average of 10 hours work per day. There is a fluctuation in the request for labor power bound to seasons. For instance, the building sector needs few labor in the rainy season; at that time women are forced to loan for getting food.
In this segment of the labor market age plays also an important role: mainly young and strong women work in the construction sector where the daily wages are relatively high. Getting older and weakened by delivering children, the construction work is too severe. So they are forced to earn their money with small trading on the street. The earnings are going down, working hours are going up but the work is less severe. They can do their job while they are sitting and do not have to toil sandbags or stones in the burning sun.

The possibility of investment is the most important criterion for differences between the sections of the informal labor market. Another essential factor forms the availability of a network of contacts. Women with contacts can create a secure work situation for themselves, others have to find a way of living from day to day.

5.1.2 Unpaid or shadow labor

Unpaid labor besides paid work

Unpaid labor and paid work is classified in four different groups. These groups form a spectrum from unpaid labor to paid labor: I. household labor, II. money saving labor, III. family labor, and IV. individual labor.

According to this spectrum a significant distinction between two major groups of respondents is obvious:
1. women, who do paid labor besides their unpaid basic tasks (groups III and IV); and
2. women who do only unpaid and money saving labor (groups I and II).

The life cycle stage influence the position in the labor spectrum too. (See table 5.1 and paragraph 5.1.3).
Mothers of dependent children work very often unpaid: every day again they need three to seven hours fetching water, graining raki or rice, washing and cooking twice. The amount of work hours depends on the distance to the water source, dry or wet season, technology and the fuel used by cooking.
Female heads of households, doing these basic survival tasks besides paid work, are forced to use less hours per day (3-6 hours) than women, not working for money (5-7 hours).

With or without husband

The research results show also a distinction between female workers with and without a husband. Respondents who are head of the household (no husband

around) spend less time unpaid. If they have a well-paid job, housework is done by servants or family members. If respondents work on heavy and badly paid jobs, few housekeeping is done. Some employers give daily cooked food as pay in kind (water carriers, servants). Food shops along the street are serving others. Food preparing, children caring and housekeeping are limited to a survival minimum: it takes only two hours per day.
Women with a husband need more time for unpaid tasks. They have to keep a household in which the husband enjoys service, but he takes no or little housework upon his shoulder. A husband costs women one to two hours unpaid work per day extra.

Family versus individual based work

Table 5.2 shows even more that women working in family labor use one to two hours per day more for unpaid care than women working paid on individual base. An important characteristic of women working in family labor is the coincidence of their living place and the place where they work for money. For them the combination of paid and unpaid work is more simply; there is no distance to bridge.

Family labor

The total number of worked hours per day is the highest for respondents who work in family labor and have dependent children. They work between fourteen and seventeen hours per day, of which six hours is done unpaid.
The standard of living of the households in this group is relative high (Rs 300-1000 per month). The labor market model (figure 5.2) describes their position: family labor is done as private initiator with investments. Examples of this kind of activities are laundries or tailor workshops with fixed customers, or the keeping of cattle for milk production. In this way one labor hour makes more money than hours worked without skill or access to capital and contacts. On the other hand 'investment' often leads to taking risks and the chance to failure. Debts to moneylenders and banks is a frequent problem in this group.

Individual labor

Within the group of respondents who have the same family circumstances, but work on individual paid base, on the average, women are working two and a half hour per day less, but there is a significant lower standard of living (Rs 150 per month). These women are working at the second segment of the labor markets (figure 5.2). Often there is no male breadwinner, so women alone earn the household income. Between two and five persons have to live from this income. The female head of the household is forced to sell her labor for extreme unfavorable prices.

Unpaid and money saving labor

Respondents without any paid employment (groups I and II) can be split up in two categories: the hidden unemployed, and women who do not need (or want) paid employment. Few women in Hosur can permit the luxury of being only housewife. The majority of well-educated wives of men with a fixed income subcontract their household duties to servants or family members and stay in their paid employment if possible. This choice for paid employment is necessary because of the high cost of living in Hosur, while low wages domestics and the availability of mothers (-in-law) and single aunts, willing to take over the house keeping, makes this possible.

Lack of paid employment force women in group II to sell their labor power for some food and shelter. Others try to save some food for a daily family meal from petty commodity trade in vegetables. These women end up every day with the same twenty, twenty-five rupees as they started in the morning with more or less the same small amount of (borrowed) money. Some poor women in Hosur try to cultivate vegetables in kitchen gardens around the house. Family of rural migrants in Hosur sometimes send once a year a part of the 'raki' or 'paddy' harvest. The total lack of education, capital and public support limits opportunities for better life.

5.1.3 Women's work and life cycle

For making a further analysis of the labor market model it is important to pay attention to the different stages in the life cycle of women. The concept life cycle is important for determining the time women need for managing their household. The life cycle can be divided in three stages:

1. the period in which women do not take care of children,
2. the period in which they have to look after their children very intensive, and
3. the period in which they are carried through their household obligations by the assistance of older children.

All interviewed women do unpaid work to a larger or smaller extent (see table 5.1 and 5.2). Without this type of work, survival in Hosur would be virtually impossible. Its semi-peripheral character determines the labor intensity of living in this fast growing town.

Deficient public services make (drinking) water a very labor-intensive article, just like food and clothing. The division of labor between the sexes makes many of these basic tasks 'women's work'. This kind of work has priority over paid work: only when basic necessities have been provided by (other) women, respondents can dedicate time to paid jobs.

5.2 Viewpoint of life expectations

5.2.1 Accessibility of the paid labor market

The preceding text shows the differentiation and mobility of the labor market in Hosur. It is useless to give a single interpretation regarding the accessibility of paid labor for women. With the help of the labor market models (figure 5.1 and

Table 5.1 Composition of the sample in Hosur

Stage in life cycle	Position in the labor spectrum				
	I	II	III	IV	Total
1:young women without children	1	1	2	13	17
2:women + dependent children	-	5	6	5	16
3:women + independent children	2	1	4	10	17
total	3	7	12	28	50

Source: own survey 1986.

I. household labor
II. moneysaving labor
III. family labor
IV. individual labor

Table 5.2 Average number of working hours per day per respondent

Labor combination average hours/day per respondent:	Position in the labor spectrum: unpaid labor: house-hold labor	money-saving labor	paid labor: family labor	individual labor	N
	I	II	III	IV	
Life cycle 1					17
unpaid hours	4	4	4	1	
paid hours	0	3	3.5	8.4	
total hours	4	7	7.5	9.4	
Life cycle 2					16
unpaid hours	-	10.8	6	4	
paid hours	-	1	9.25	8.75	
total hours	-	11.8	15.75	12.75	
Life cycle 3					17
unpaid hours	5	5	4.25	3	
paid hours	2	4.5	7.45	9.75	
total hours	7	9.5	11.7	12.75	
N	3	7	12	28	50

Source: own survey 1986.

5.2) and a simple overview of indicators (table 5.3) it is possible to formulate an idea of the interrelations (horizontal and vertical) of the labor market sections. As indicators for structuring the labor markets, we choose 'caste', 'education', 'migration background' and 'stage in life cycle'. During the research it turned out that also other indicators as 'possibility of investment' and 'network of contacts' are important (see table 5.3).

If we want to know which mobility exists between the segments, the labor market models are too static. Furthermore they do not show the combinations of labor categories women can make per day. The labor markets in Hosur look more like a mountainous landscape, with two tops (of the formal labor market and informal labor market) lying at a bottom of shadow labor (see figure 5.3). Mobility is frequent between the lower segments but the 'aristocracy' at the top of the formal and informal mountains are not willing to let in strangers (Harriss, 1986).

Table 5.3 Indicators for status of women at the paid labor market

Indicators	Formal labor market segments: I	II	III	Informal labor market segments: Ii	IIi	IIIi
Caste	+	+/-	-	+	+/-	-
Migration	u	u	u/r	r	r	r
Life cycle	1/3	1	1/3	2/3	2/3	2/3
Education	++	+	+/-	+/-	-	-
Investment	+	+	-	+	-	-
Contacts	++	+	+	+	-	-

Caste: + =forward; +/- =forward/backward; - =backward/scheduled
migration background: u = urban, r = rural, u/r = both
Life cycle: 1 =no child; 2 = dependent child; 3 = ind. children
Education/ Investment/ Contacts: ++ = good, + = medium;
+/- = little; - = none)

Source: own survey 1986.

Walls around the area of permanent wage labor are rather thick. One only comes through if he or she has disposal of a good educational level, money to invest and contacts. For the top of the informal labor mountain the same applies; only the formal education level is less important. It is more the training in practice someone needs on the informal labor mountain.

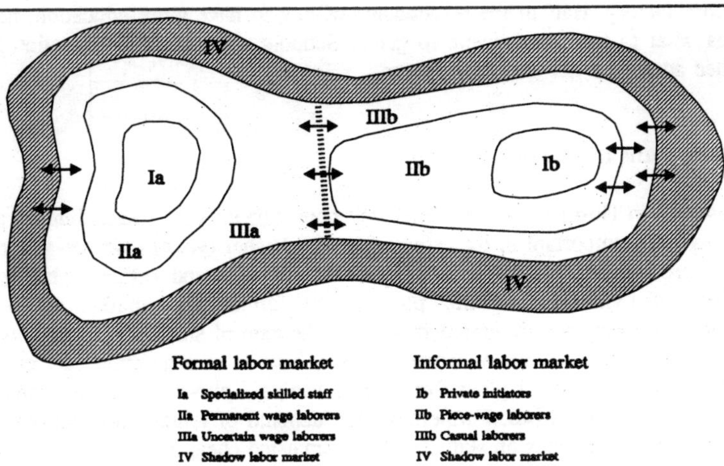

Figure 5.3 Segmented labor markets as labor mountains for women in Hosur. Outline according to Breman, Bromley and Holmström.

5.2.2 Mobility at the labor mountains

In this paragraph we will describe the factual and desirable forms of mobility at the labor markets. Half of the women of our research gives priority to their unpaid tasks in life. If it was economically realizable, one third of the women who do paid work, would like to stop 'working' and spend their energy and time on housekeeping and child care. However most women (86%) work seven or more hours per day for money. Most of them (63%) are forced to combine their unpaid and paid labor. For nearly one-third, paid work does have a priority over unpaid work. 37% of all women is pleased to make a combination of paid and unpaid labor in their lives.

Upwards mobility

Only five women (10%) improved their employment actually, these are a highly skilled telegrapher, a stenographer and a data typist, an older shopkeeper with independent children and a dohbi. These women have no common characteristics except that they are free from daily poverty and possess a strong health and character and are already active at the paid labor market. Best help to get a better job is recommendations, according to the respondents. Money and time to invest are also important resources as is the support of their husband or father. It is extremely difficult for women to act in public without the permission of dominant male family members. Education is of minor importance, according to the women. The women who want to get more education, prefer general education in basics: to read and write, bookkeeping and industrial training for work in a factory. Half of the respondents willing to have more education, have no idea what to learn and where to get it. Schools with informal education for unskilled adults are not known in Hosur.

5.2.3 Life paths of women

The research in Hosur shows the trend that poor women with small children are becoming more important in the informal sector. Richer (young) women without children are working in the formal sector of factories and offices. The rigid separation of living and working place at the formal labor market makes it impossible to combine paid employment with the care of small children at once. Mothers, employed as typist or factory worker, have to arrange child care or are forced to resign. Public or other forms of collectively nursery near the working place do not exist in Hosur. Furthermore the demand of female laborers for the formal sector concentrates on skilled young unmarried cheap workers.
The separation of living and working place is less present at the informal labor market. This is one of the decisive reasons why mothers of children will find suitable employment on the informal market. For caring tasks these mothers get support from their grown-up children and other members of the household.
If subcontracting relations exist, the work is brought to the living place. In or around the own house it is done by all possible family members on piece rate base. In the case of self-employment the living function is brought to the working place. In both cases the mix of living and working functions on one place makes it possible to combine the caring and income-generating tasks. To illustrate these combinations we have made three daily paths of women, who are mothers and have to earn money. Time-use and life history methods developed by Hägerstrand (1979) and Carlstein (1982) are used.

> *I Combination living/working place*
> *Rana Navamaku works at home, with her mother-in-law and her sister-in-law. Her two small children are playing around, but are not allowed to touch the toxic substance of which Rana rolls the incense sticks. Every 1000 pieces brings in one and a half rupee. She rolls an average of 6000 per day. Her mother-in-law takes care of the meals, Rana of the children in the meantime.*
>
> *II Separation living/working place*
> *Dhana works in a factory, she leaves her baby with her neighbors, paying Rs 200 per month. When Dhana comes home in the evening, she first picks up the baby and then cokes her meal for the next day.*
>
> *III Combination working/living place*
> *Govindamma has moved her entire family-life to her sari-sari shop along the main street of Hosur. There she is selling 13 hours per day or she is waiting for her customers. Her five children can find her there. Her three nippers scratch around the shop all-day. The thirteen year old daughter takes over a part of her mothers tasks, she collects water, brings the small children to her mother, cooks in rotation with her mother the daily meals. Furthermore the daughter earns money in construction work. The eldest son of Govindamma attends school and helps his mother in the afternoon the merchandise.*

Constraints of women's life

Organizing the household is depending on the different possibilities to provide a living. Restricting factors are the kind of work which is accessible, the possibility to arrange public nursery and the required quality of housekeeping. Other factors are the personal taste and ruling ideology regarding to motherhood and working outside the home. In the diverse situations different organization of the household will be the most effective.

> *Because Rana failed to pass her last exam at school, just before she was married, she is not qualified for a factory job. Her husband wants her to work along in the production of incense-sticks, in which he works as a middleman. Rana despises the situation, she feels kept hostage by her family-in-law. But she loves her children. When her husband proposed sterilization after the second child (a son), she refused. She wants another child. In the month she is going to give birth, she will return to her native place and stay with her mother for three months. May be she is able to study the profession of tailor. As tailor Rana gets rid of incense-stick rolling.*

Although remote from what she wants, Rana chooses this combination of home-based work and taking care of her small children; it provides the most perspective for the life she wants: namely three children and work as a tailor.
Dhana is restricted in another field. Her formal contract at the factory (Rs 850

per month) enables her the luxury of paid nursery and housekeeping. She pays Rs 200 on this, so she has Rs 650 left for living and saving.

> *No family member is available to take care of Dhana's baby. Because Dhana entered into love-marriage with the husband she choose, she was renounced by her own family and by her family-in-law. Her husband earns not enough to live together. Moreover he is working in another town. She does not like the situation. Most women give her the cold-shoulder, because she lives alone with her child, working six days per week, while there is nobody at home to take care of the baby and the household.*

In the case of Govindamma there is only one main objective: how to get a daily meal for the family. The husband of Govindamma brings home irregularly some money. He works as a coolie in the construction work, but not every day and an important part of the earnings is spend by himself on coffee and beedies.[6]
Govindamma has given birth to five children. After the deliveries her back is too weak for construction work. Like many other hard working women Govindamma suffers from uterus infections after her sterilization. Being a Harijan, a woman and Kannada-speaking, paid labor is hard to find in Hosur, which is oriented at Telugu and Tamil language. For her only petty trade (in her own community) is left over to earn money.

> *In cooperation with other merchant women in her neighborhood Govindamma started to trade in vegetables. She got a loan for a sari-sarishop[7] through a special arrangement for Harijans. From the Rs 1000, Rs 700 has been paid off in amounts of Rs 35 per month. Her customers are living in the same district as Govindamma. It is called Perinagar, built by rural migrants themselves on squatted ground. They are living from day to day. If necessary Govindamma sells on tick. Mostly Govindamma is well supplied: bananas, leaves, ginger, coriander, tomatoes, unions and some potatoes. Her customers spend daily a half or one rupee. If they run out of money, they put a stripe behind their names, writing in the note-book of Govindamma. They will pay later on, in better times.*

For Govindamma and so many other street traders the profit is low. Working 12 to 13 hours per day, she earns Rs 90 per month and the vegetables, left over daily. Govindamma is the lowest paid worker among the respondents, with most working hours. However this way of living and working is the most profitable,

---

[6] Kalpagam (1983) and Gulati (1981) describe the difference in behavior of men and women in the same household. Men are spending 66% of their cash income on coffee, food and liquor for themselves. Women spend most of their income on food for their family. Their income in kind (in the case of servants, dohbi's and water carriers) forms the basic food for the children (Schenk-Sandbergen, 1982).

[7] Hackenberg and Barth (1984) describe the possibilities for money making and upward mobility for sari-sarishops keepers and defend the idea that small-scale women vendors must get governmental support.

given the fact that there is no employment at all for women like Govindamma in Hosur. Now she is able to combine the care for her children and earning a living for her family. She is part of an active community and performs a social role. The left-overs of her trade ensure the daily meals of her family.

More research is needed on the organization of the household economics. The available data lead to the conclusion that the circumstances determine most efficient combination of paid, money saving and unpaid labor. In the case of unskilled women with dependent children in Hosur the informal labor market offers more paid employment than the formal labor market.

Combinations of different types of work

On an individual level, we looked at the combinations of categories of work women do in Hosur. Four different types, chosen from a women's specific place on the labor spectrum and life cycle were compiled into a day scheme.

I. The supervisor (life cycle stage 1) working in a factory of electronics combines the following in an average day:

8 hours permanent wage labor	(33%)
1 hour hidden wage labor	(4%)
2.5 hours unpaid family work	(10%)
0.5 hour travel time	(2%)
2 hours leisure time	(8%)
10 hours sleep	(42%)
------------------------------	-----
24 hours a day	100%

II. The teacher with a baby and a mother at home who takes care of the baby (life cycle stage 3) combines the following in an average day:

8 hours permanent wage labor	(33%)
2.5 hours self-employment	(10%)
3 hours unpaid family work	(13%)
1 hour commuting	(4%)
1 hour leisure time	(4%)
8.5 hours sleep	(35%)
------------------------------	-----
24 hours a day	100%

III. The water-carrier, with a mentally deficient daughter and a twelve year old son, (life cycle stage 3) working on the building-site:

7.5 hours hidden wage labor	(31%)
3 hours dependent labor	(12%)
3.5 hours unpaid family work	(15%)
10 hours sleep	(42%)
------------------------------	-----
24 hours a day	100%

IV. The vegetable-seller, with three dependent children and two independent children: a 13-year old daughter who helps with unpaid and paid work and a 10-year old son who goes to school (life cycle stage 2), she spends:

14	hours unstable self-employment	(58%)
1.5	hour unpaid family work	(6%)
1	hour travel time	(4%)
7.5	hours sleep	(31%)
24	hours a day	100%

Comparing the (paid) working hours with the income gives us the earned profit in table 5.4.

Table 5.4 (Paid) working hours compared with income

% Time spend at paid work and profit

% time/day	profit
Supervisor :37% a day	600 Rs/month, 28 days
Teacher :43% a day	775 Rs/month, 22 days, 300 Rs in self-empl.
Waterlady :43% a day	360 Rs/month, 30 days, 120 Rs in food
Veg-seller :58% a day	90 Rs/month, 30 days, + food

Time: Respondent	%/day unpaid	%/day paid	per hour profit	%/day traveling	working time total
Supervisor	8	37	2.4 Rs	2	47%
Teacher	12	43	3.3 Rs	4	59%
Waterlady	14	43	1.15 Rs	-	57%
Veg-seller	6	58	0.21 Rs	4	68%

Source: own survey 1986.

The time women spend on unpaid work for the family (caring and money-saving activities) is dependent on the composition of the household and the amount of time remaining after the daily paid work. Not only the number of children determine the amount of time a mother must invest in house-keeping, but the age and sex of the children are also a crucial factor. An older daughter can take over a lot of household tasks from the mother (see the vegetable-seller), whereas an older son will try to earn some money for the household. Looking at the division of labor in the household of the waterlady the gender-specific roles become clear. Her oldest daughter is mentally ill and can not give any help. The older son is not 'used' to take over the housekeeping, so he tries to get work on the building-site. Salema, the waterlady, has to spend the most time (15%) on unpaid housekeeping.

The distance between home and work plays an important role: travelling takes time, unpaid time. The amount of time is dependent on the distance and the means of travel. The cultural barrier which makes it impossible for women to ride bicycles, implies more traveling time for women in Hosur. But more important is the fact that the combination of categories of work (caring for small children and earning a living) is only possible in the categories where living place and working place are the same. This is the case in self-employment, and sometimes in dependent and hidden wage-labor categories.

Jobs in the formal labor market separate working place (factory, office) and living place (home). So all the mothers with dependent children who want to work formally, need a baby-sitter or an arrangement. It is clear that the full combination of labor categories results in the lowest profit in money per hour: long working days with low profit.

5.3 Conclusions

Growth pole policy could create employment for women, provided that applied education is accessible for women and there are facilities of favorable credit allowance for women only[8].

The vertical accessibility at the formal labor market is restricted. Between the segments there is a high barrier of education level, investment and contacts. Furthermore the division of living and working place makes the combination of paid and unpaid work at once impossible. Mothers without the help of public or family nursery are forced to make such combinations.
Female employees at the hills and top of the formal labor mountain migrated from urban environments. They have applied for one of the available women's jobs at the formal labor market. Given the fact that there are only a few female labor factories in and around Hosur (electronics and fruit canning) the market is filled quickly.

Besides the vertical accessibility at the informal labor market there is a significant horizontal flexibility between the lowest segments of the informal labor market, the grey zone and the lowest segments of the formal labor market. For most women in Hosur paid employment is only accessible in the gray zone between formal and informal sector and at the bottom of the informal labor market. The division lines between these sections of the labor market are flexible and women are used to fit in the possibilities and necessaries at that time.
The payments in the several segments and the required level of education diverge not much. An advantage compared with the informal employment is the extent of income security of the formal labor market. Even if the payment is low, the security makes this kind of employment desirable in the eyes of women who need a certain source of income.

Female home based and casual workers get better employment when the work of middleman and labor broker are taken over by themselves. In that case they have control over their own labor and the earnings. The division line between the second and the first segments of the informal labor market are so drawn less firm, and women (alone or in cooperation) can operate as initiators on the informal labor market.

Contrary to the aims of growth pole policy, especial rural migrants and local women have hardly benefits of this policy. In Hosur they are forced to take the marginal work, left over by men. Compared with the position of women in

[8] If credit facilities are sexe-neutral, men push female lenders away.

peasant communities their life becomes more uncertain, and their position even more marginal. Women in Hosur are pushed in a male dominated urban labor system, and are only used as lubricant for the machinery. In this way the current growth pole policy cannot be called an improvement for women's life.

6. Unskilled Labor in Hosur

Angeline Ackermans, Johan Beth, Gerard Keune and Femme Riemersma

The establishment of large-scale industrial companies with a technological advanced production process, resulted in a strong growth of employment, mainly for skilled laborers. Not only in SIPCOT and SIDCO companies, but also in the non-registered workshops, of which a number existed already before SIPCOT and SIDCO companies came. Most of the workshops has been founded after economic activity in Hosur increased. It is doubtful if the rapidly growing number of economic activities has been beneficial for the unskilled laborers. The labor-conditions, e.g. wages, employment security and amount of working hours, may not be improved or deteriorated.
The growing amount of construction activities in Hosur attracted a large number of unskilled laborers. The demand for unskilled labor is not sufficient to supply a job for every incoming migrant. This labor reserve probably influences the labor-conditions, especially wage, in a negative way. Presumably there will be no difference in labor-conditions for unskilled laborers working either in a capitalist or a semi-capitalist company or with traditional tradesmen. It will be of more importance what the relation is to the labor contractor.
Although women are working outside the family circle in all kinds of areas, it appears that a large number works in the unorganized sector. Of this amount a large percentage works in the construction industry. The position of the female construction worker is very strong influenced by the family situation. The combination of work inside and outside the home will depend on the amount of work that the family requires. (See also chapter 5).
This chapter has been divided into three main sections. Firstly attention will be paid to the role of unskilled labor in the modern factories and the more traditional workshops (6.1). The next section (6.2) analyses the traditional and modern construction sector. In 6.3 the unskilled male and female construction laborers are the central subject of study. In the final part (6.4) some conclusions will be drawn.

6.1 Unskilled labor in modern industry and workshops

In this section attention will be focussed on those laborers in industry and workshops, who perform unskilled labor. Unskilled labor has been defined as labor for which no special training, education or knowledge is required by the worker and which can be done by anyone at any time. This group of workers does certainly not correspond to unskilled workers. Especially in big companies (SIPCOT, SIDCO) unskilled labor appears not to be done by unskilled people. Mainly this relates to the large labor supply in Hosur. To make a comparison

possible between workers from all types of companies, a definition of laborers who perform unskilled labor had to be chosen.
Two questions are important:
- What are the labor-conditions of workers who perform unskilled labor?
- What are the possibilities to improve the labor-conditions?

Labor-conditions consist of working hours, security, wages, bonuses, labor-satisfaction and labor organization. Labor-conditions are determined by a number of factors:
1. factors relating to the position of the individual worker like age, education.
2. factors of political nature, like labor legislation.
3. factors which influence the structure of the labor market like type and size of the company.

A categorization has been made of the companies from which workers were selected. This classification is based on the kind of influence the factory is exercising. For companies with 50 workers or more the Factory Act gives detailed labor-conditions. For companies with 10 to 50 workers the Factories Act is less detailed, as for companies with less than 10 workers does not apply. Holmström (1984) refers to the relation between size of the company and economic conditions of the worker. The organized sector has higher wages, more labor-security, more labor organization and protection by labor-legislation than the non-organized sector. Next to it a number of sectors of companies have been chosen, namely those sector with a lot of unskilled labor, with a lot of companies in Hosur and with companies in all size-categories. These sectors are: food and tobacco, general engineering, transport, electronics and building materials. Differences in labor-conditions between sectors are too small and accidental to set much value on. Differences between categories on the other hand are substantial. Three categories are distinguished, based on the classification of Harriss (1982) with a few minor adjustments. For the workers from the selected companies only Harriss' first two categories are important (see chapter 2); the second category will be split up.

I. permanent wage workers: workers from SIPCOT and SIDCO companies who have a letter of appointment and earn less than Rs 1000 a month.

II. short-term wage workers in registered companies: workers from SIPCOT and SIDCO firms who have no letter of appointment.

III. short-term wage workers in unregistered small firms: workers from other companies than SIPCOT and SIDCO companies (mostly from small workshops) who have no letter of appointment.

Group I is the organized sector, group II and III constitute the unorganized sector. The permanent wage workers are proportionately more unionized, have on the average better wages, better secondary labor-conditions, reasonable working hours and a fairly good labor-security. The registered short-term wage workers have managed to get a job within SIPCOT and SIDCO companies, but as far as wages and secondary labor-conditions are concerned, they are well behind workers from category I. In many cases wages are even lower than those of workers in category III, where years of experience might lead to reasonable wages. Main point for this category of workers remains their labor-security. As long as they do not get a letter of appointment, their position will be unstable. Besides, in Tamil Nadu there is no longer a term in which a worker should be given a letter of appointment. In view of their unstable position and low wages, labor satisfaction amongst these workers is very low.

For the unregistered short-term wage workers there is no labor-legislation, they are not unionized, have low wages, long working hours and have a poor education. It is remarkable that these workers have very little ambition to work in SIPCOT and SIDCO companies. This shows their sense of reality, because in view of their poor education these workers have few chances in the registered companies. The poor education does certainly not mean that they have no professional skills; some of them have even ambition to start their own workshop. It is also striking that these workers are fairly satisfied about their labor-security. Very few workers were afraid to lose their jobs. They argued: "As long as we do a fine job, the boss won't have a reason to fire us."

6.1.1 Characteristics and labor-conditions of the workers

Education plays a peculiar part with the different labor-categories. In table 6.1[1] one can see a summary of the workers' education:

Table 6.1 Education of the workers

category	education		
	none	< standard IX	≥ standard IX
I	4%	24%	72%
II	19%	31%	50%
III	18%	64%	18%

Source: own survey 1985.

Education has no importance for the type of work that has to be done, but on the other hand it is very important with getting a job in SIPCOT and SIDCO companies. The huge labor supply, mentioned before, will account for this.
One marked difference between the categories is formed by religion. In table 6.2 one can see the high percentage of muslims in category III; many workshops in category III were owned by muslims, who preferred muslim-workers; also family-ties were important.

In table 6.3 one can see that many workers from category I came from far away (for instance from the Madras area). Often the companies they worked with had ties with companies from big cities, e.g. Madras.
The age differences between the three categories of workers are slight. The average age in category I is 27.7 years, in category II 24.2 years and in category III 22.1 years.

[1] Standard IX is the beginning of junior secondary school; after Standard XII this may lead to the Secondary School Leavers' Certificate; in category I 32% had the SSLC, in category II and III resp. 6% and 9%.

Table 6.2 Religion of the workers

category	religion		
	hindu	muslim	christian
I	88%	8%	4%
II	75%	13%	13%
III	45%	55%	0%

Source: own survey 1985.

Table 6.3 Place of origin of the workers

category	place of origin		
	Hosur taluk	Dharmapuri or adjacent district	from elsewhere
I	32%	32%	36%
II	50%	19%	31%
III	55%	27%	18%

Source: own survey 1985.

In table 6.4 a summary of the working hours is given. A clear distinction between categories I and II on the one hand and category III on the other can be observed. All the workers in the first two categories have a regular working week of six days, eight hours a day. The unregistered short-term wage workers show a rather diverse number of working hours per week.

Table 6.4 Working hours of the worker[2]

category	number of working hours per week								
	48	54	57	60	70	72	84	98	irregular
I	100%								
II	100%								
III	37%	10%	7%	7%	7%	7%	17%	3%	6,6%

Source: own survey 1985.

The average wage per month in category I is Rs 617, in category II Rs 208 and in category III Rs 298. These last two figures seem rather odd, but when one takes into account that in category III working hours are approximately 40% longer than in category II, wages in both categories are almost the same. The height of the wages is associated with a number of explaining factors[3] in a regression analysis, as can be seen from table 6.5.

Striking is the important relation of the letter of appointment with the income level. The only advantage registered short-term wage workers have, is the fact that they might get a letter of appointment with all matching advantages. Unregistered short-term wage workers do not have this opportunity.

Concerning the secondary labor-conditions, marked differences between the three categories were found. In category I all the workers have official secondary labor-conditions like dearness allowance, insurance, etc.; in category II only 50%, while in category III nobody receives this type of allowances.

[2] Irregular may be more or less than 48 hours.

[3] Education seemed not important in explaining height of wages but is, as we have seen before, of great importance in determining in which category one works.

Table 6.5 Factors explaining the height of the wages

independent factor	% of the wages that is explained				
	by 1	by 1,2	by 1,2,3	by 1-4	by 1-5
1 letter of appointment	41.6%				
2 age		52.6%			
3 labor service			57.7%		
4 category				59.2%	
5 sector					60.3%

Source: own survey 1985.

Finally we will focus on the level of organization of the laborers. In category I 52% of the workers is unionized, in contrast with the categories II and III with not any form of labor-organization. It should be noted that the majority of the unionized workers is member of a management-union. Such a union has been formed and is controlled by the management of the company. Only 29% of the unionized workers were members of real trade-unions or workers-unions.
Permanent wage workers can only hope that unions can secure better labor-conditions for them; their chance for promotion is small. This takes us to the second question, namely what are the possibilities to improve the labor-conditions.

6.1.2 Possibilities to improve labor-conditions

A proceeding unionization may play an important role in the improvement of the labor-conditions of the workers in the unskilled sector in Hosur. At present many companies try to prevent unionization by banning it completely or by creating unions controlled by the management of the company.
Solidarity amongst workers has to increase in order to be able to make demands. Workers-unions are quite good for this purpose. Trade-unions might appear later, for showing that existing labor-legislation is evaded, or by demonstrating the shortcomings of the labor-legislation.
Because labor-supply is more than sufficient, it will be difficult to promote solidarity. Above that one can wonder whether trade-unions have enough power in India. Ramaswamy and Ramaswamy (1981) are moderately optimistic; they notice that no trade-union in India, tied to any political party, has lost its independence with regard to the party. Would this happen, than the union will lose sight of its main goal: "To defend as good as possible, the interests of the workers, even if they go against political interests". (Ramaswamy and Ramaswamy 1981, p. 128).

Indeed it often appears that when trade-unions are working within companies they operate very uncoordinated, so it is quite possible for companies to sow discord between groups of workers. This weakens the position of the workers is very much.

For registered short-term wage workers it is very important that Tamil Nadu again introduces the maximum term a worker may be employed without a letter of appointment (this term has been abolished after severe pressure on the state government by the employers).

The unregistered short-term wage worker will not notice anything of these improvements as long as the labor-legislation does not count for him. In the case of big workshops, ways will be found to evade the rules, for example by dividing the workshop into small units with less than 10 workers each. There is no indication that the labor-legislation will also be applied to small workshops. Here exploitation of the workers can continue undisturbedly. These workers have to find a different answer. Partly this answer came already forward when a lot of them explained that they wished to start their own workshop in the near future. For many of them this will be impossible, due to lack of finance. A solution might be to start a cooperative business, a company controlled by the workers themselves. Often a cooperation can find access to financial means. Moreover workers will not be exploited any longer within their company.

6.2 The construction sector

The construction sector forms an important part of the economy and can be seen as a stimulating force in the developing process in Third World countries (Moavenzadeh 1978, Stretton 1979 and Ramachandran 1980). Its importance is that it has a function in the material and social satisfaction of needs and the stimulating of the economic growth through forward and backward linkages. Specially Ramachandran (1980) sees a role for the building sector as stimulator of the growth of employment. The construction sector can, if the right techniques and materials are used, make use of the big potential of labor forces. Projects who are simple could give a big number of unskilled laborers a job, who otherwise would have been unemployed.
The construction material and maintenance industries can also use semi- or unskilled laborers and give them an on-the-job training. Construction labor may help in developing leadership and managerial skills as it has done traditionally in the more developed countries.

Besides these positive sides of the working in the construction sector also a few negative sides are mentioned in the literature. The irregular supply of work, the related labor uncertainty and the necessary spatial mobility of the laborers have to be mentioned. The absence of a long-term contract relieves the employer of the insurance, sickness and maternity benefits etc. For the worker this system is exploitative. Wages are low and irregular, so that they cannot be relied upon or planned for. The uncertainty of the employment provides ideal circumstances for corruption (Blake 1982).

In this paragraph we will discuss the effects of the government policies concerning housing on the structure of the building materials market. Not only the materials but also the producers in the building sector will be influenced by the expansion of the building activities. Special attention will be paid to the position of the small-scale builders. Firstly we pay attention to the traditional and modern construction sector in Hosur. In the following paragraph we will analyze the changes in the building materials market as a result of the growth in the number of building projects. Then we will do the same for the small-scale builders in relation to the changing building materials market.

6.2.1 Traditional and modern construction in Hosur

The expansion of the housing stock is one of the consequences of Hosur's growth pole policy. The government is the main builder of houses and therefore influences the building materials market. Several modern, relatively expensive materials have been introduced. Only a few retailers in Hosur monopolize the market and create an artificial scarcity. The high demand of materials with a better quality like cement and steel, is a reason for the government to control the prices and/or the distribution. Private clients are able to buy (a limited amount of) materials for a fixed price. However the price levelling created a black market circuit, where the higher income groups can buy all materials they need.
Traditional materials got more competition from the new materials. One could expect price reduction, but because of the expanding market the demand for traditional materials grew and the prices raised.
The new materials are accompanied by new building techniques. In general the small-scale producers do not have the knowledge to work with innovative techniques and are therefore not able to execute projects for the government and for the private clients, who want to use the new building system. Small-scale contractors can only work in government projects as a subcontractor. Because of their lack of knowledge, the small-scale contractors are getting more dependent on large-scale contractors. Further price fluctuations of the materials may also affect the position of small-scale contractors. Price increase of traditional materials means that many, especially low income, builders cannot afford to buy the materials and are therefore not able to build more. This means less work for the small-scale contractors in this segment of the building market. In the extending housing market there is more work to all the contractors, but it is very difficult for the small-scale contractors to remain independent.

6.2.2 The building materials market

A distinction can be made between the traditional and the modern building materials. Examples of traditional materials are sun-burned bricks, yellistone, palmthatch, lime, etc. They originate from the surroundings of Hosur, while modern materials like cement and steel come from large-scale factories not found in Hosur. We will pay attention to two aspects of each material, 'production' and 'distribution'.

<u>Production</u>

An important characteristic of the production process of the modern material forms the independence of seasonal fluctuations. Traditional materials, locally produced in medium-sized and small-scale production units, do depend upon the weather. Sun-burned bricks for example cannot be produced in periods of rain.

<u>Distribution</u>

The distribution of modern materials is predominantly organized by wholesalers. Only two retailers can be found in Hosur, as a result there is hardly any competition. A consequence of this lack of competition is a higher price level, with extreme high prices in periods of scarcity. The government regulates the prices and/or the distribution of certain products, e.g. cement. 60% of the cement production is used or distributed by the government for a lower price than the other 40%, which can be bought on the free market for a maximum price. However, in periods of scarcity black market activities play an even more important role.

Traditional materials are in general distributed directly to the users. Their market is highly competitive with a more stable price level. Increases in prices only arise when the unfavorable weather conditions prohibit production. The expansion of the building activities changed the building materials market. The demand for more traditional materials grew steadily, but was not as high as it could have been without the introduction of new materials like steel, cement or plastics. The government, in particular the 'Tamil Nadu Housing Board', the 'Public Works Department' and the 'New Town Development Authority' as most important institutions, played an important role in this process. The rise in demand for traditional materials also meant a rise in the prices, which lowered the accessibility of these markets for the low income groups. The modern materials were no solution, because of the higher quality and the relatively high prices. Table 8.4 gives an impression of the rise in the prices and the difference between the government and the private price levels.

Table 6.6 Price development of some building materials

material	prices in the government sector 1980 (1)	1984 (2)	prices in the private sector 1984 (3)
CEMENT	24 Rs/bag	50 Rs/bag	75- 85 Rs/bag
STEEL	2,700 Rs/MT	5,300 Rs/MT	6,000- 6,500 Rs/MT
BRICKS	180 Rs/1000p	200 Rs/1000p	250- 300 Rs/1000p
TEAKWOOD	-	-	10,600-12,400 Rs/m3
COUNTRYWOOD	2,500 Rs/m3	-	5,000- 5,500 Rs/m3
R.R.B. (4)	35 Rs/m3	-	48 Rs/m3
YELLISTONE	25 Rs/m3	-	32 Rs/m3
SAND	20 Rs/m3	-	27 Rs/m3

(1) Source: TNHB Lead Statement 1980
(2) Medium price accounted by the TNHB
(3) Prices Oct.-Nov. 1984 (rainy period)
(4) Random Rouble Boulders

6.2.3 The role of small-scale builders

In the construction sector of Hosur a number of actors are of importance: the entrepreneurs, the client and the laborers.

The entrepreneurs can be divided in three groups:

(1) The first group is the group of the big entrepreneurs, mainly formed by the contractors.

(2) The group of the small entrepreneurs is formed by the hutmakers.

(3) Between these two types is a big group of middle great entrepreneurs. These are called the mistries.

A distinction can be made between 'full contractors' and 'labor contractors'[4]. Full contractors work as the main- or as a sub-contractor and have sufficient financial possibilities to realize an entire medium-sized project. The four full contractors in Hosur are all educated as Civil Engineers and are therefore able to design projects. On their building projects it is more common to use machines, like concrete mixers and elevators. In general they are dealing with more than one project at the same time. The main part of their job is to supervise their foremen and laborers. The turn-over of all the full contractors is more than Rs 100,000 per year.

The labor contractors (or 'mistris') on the other hand mainly operate as subcontractors for private investors and full contractors. They do not use machines and acquire their knowledge by means of a 'learning by doing' process. Often they start as a coolie, from there some climb up to the position of (independent) mason, i.e. labor contractor.

The dependency of the mistris upon the main contractor is not very clear. Often they work regularly for the same contractor. One cannot easily determine whether labor contractors are really independent, or should be considered as simply employees. All the labor contractors had a turn-over lower than Rs 100,000 per year. In general they are optimistic about the possibilities of obtaining work in the near future.

The full contractors and the labor contractors can also be distinguished by their solvency. The full contractors are able to finance their projects with money from the official banks. In general they are collateral, which give the banks sufficient guarantees for lending money to them. Labor contractors have to find other ways to finance their business. They have not the possibility to borrow from banks or other financial institutions, and thus have to borrow money from family members, friends or brokers (who charge high interest rates).

The Tamil Nadu Housing Board (TNHB) is the main building initiator in Hosur. After planning the schemes and designing the infrastructure and housing blocks, the TNHB needs contractors to carry out the building process. By means of a 'tender notice' contractors who are capable of doing the desired job are invited to apply. Every interested contractor has to prove in advance their financial position.

As a consequence the labor contractors have no access to this important segment of the building market. However, they do carry out a main part of the work on the government projects. The main contractors hire labor contractors for certain parts of the job, though officially they are not allowed to subcontract parts of the projects to other unregistered contractors. In this way it is possible to spread the high risks, caused by the fluctuating market over different contractors. In rainy periods their subcontracting relationships will be very unstable.

This also means that they are not responsible for the laborers, who temporarily lose their jobs. This subcontracting system is more profitable for the main contractors: they make the high profits, without bearing big risks. They are able to exploit the small-scale contractors, because of their better financial position and greater economic and technical knowledge.

---

[4] See for a more extensive classification of building contractors in South-India: Van der Loop, 1988.

6.3 Unskilled male and female construction labor

During the research (1985) 80 active building sites were found within Hosur. Striking is the great number of in-active building sites (37). This can be explained by two factors. Firstly the method of financing seems to be very important. Many construction projects are realized by phased financing. This means that the different construction phases are realized if the money for that particular phase is available. However, some examples of building sites can be found which are in-active for already many years.
Secondly the regular returning shortages of building materials (especially of cement and steel) acts in a slackening way to the building activities. This was strengthened by the great demand of these materials by the big government projects at that time in Hosur. The shortages of labor (specially of skilled) had also a slowing-down effect on the projects.

A distinction has been made between three types of projects. Firstly there is a clear difference between government and non-government projects. Within the non-government group there is a further subdivision into house-building and non-house-building activities. Further a classification can be made with regard to the clients. The majority of the active building sites are private projects (of which 23 belong to the housing sector and 18 to the non-housing sector). The others are public building activities (two big projects: a tax-office and a large housing scheme).
The total number of laborers working at the 43 selected active building sites is 1176 (see table 6.7).

Table 6.7 Division of laborers to kind of project

	private sector		government	total
	house-building	non-house-building		
unskilled men	60 35,1%	59 31,9%	231 28,2%	350
unskilled women	56 32,7%	74 40,0%	199 24,4%	329
skilled men	55 32,2%	52 28,1%	390 47,6%	497
total	171 100%	185 100%	820 100%	1176

Source: own survey 1985.

The next paragraphs are concerned with male and female laborers which do unskilled labor in the construction sector in Hosur[5]. The work they do consists most times of carrying activities. Also riddling of sand, sprinkling of water and preparation of cement (only the mixing) and guarding of the building site is part of their work.

[5] The minimum age of the selected laborers is 10 years. This limit is chosen because it appeared that interviewing children below this age limit is most times difficult. The research is limited to the built-up area of Hosur.

6.3.1 Personal characteristics of unskilled laborers

In this paragraph some elementary information will be given of the unskilled laborers who do unskilled work. Successively the demographic, the economic, the socio-cultural and the individual characteristics will be dealt with.

Demographic characteristics

Striking is the low age of the unskilled construction laborers, the majority of this group has an age below 30 years (see table 6.8).

Table 6.8 Age distribution of unskilled construction laborers

Age	female	male
< 20	48%	35%
20 - 30	30%	41%
30 - 40	14%	14%
40 - 50	6%	4%
> 50	2%	6%

Source: own survey 1985.

If the workers are becoming older, they participate less in the labor process. This can be explained by the fact that the construction work is very heavy and the employer will more likely hire a younger laborer. For the female laborers it is also important that after being married (often before the age of 20) the woman is in the first place responsible for the domestic affairs. Especially the non-married group consists for an important part (62%) of male laborers. There is resistance to the working of unmarried girls/women outside their own house. Because after their first menstruation they are sexual attractive and should be kept at home.

Table 6.9 The marital status

	female	male
not-married	28%	44%
married	50%	46%
widow/er	10%	4%
divorced	8%	4%
other	4%	2%

Source: own survey 1985.

Despite the low age of the respondents almost half of this group is head of the household, mainly male laborers (76%). If the father in a family dies it is not the mother but the oldest son who becomes head of the household. The male and female laborers belong to households with an average size of four persons.

Economic characteristics

The mean income per member per day for the household of female laborers is on an average Rs 1.2 lower than the comparable amount of the male laborers (Rs 5.9 and Rs 7.1 respectively). This indicates that the female respondents who are working in the construction sector are from families which are poorer than the ones of the males. These figures should however be connected with the purchasing power. It appears that 16% of the households is below the absolute poverty limit (Rs 2.75 per member per day[6]). The phase in the life-cycle appears to be very important in influencing the position of the family in relation to the absolute poverty limit. It is in particular the low age of the children which prevents the mother to participate on the labor market.

Despite the low earnings of the unskilled construction laborers, more than one-third of them could save some money. A great deal of the respondents are saving money for family-members in the native place (37%) or for costs for the school of the children, especially boys (20%). Less important is saving money for future extension of the family (14%), cloth (9%) and repayments of debts (6%). Saving money for unexpected expenses in case of unemployment or illness is also not very popular (14%). If such circumstances occur and money is needed for food or medicines, 58% of the respondents will go to the employer for money. A smaller number (32%) will try to borrow some money from family or friends. Only a minority tries to get financial 'support' from a moneylender.
If money is borrowed of the employer the repayment will normally be done by reduction of the salary. If it is a small amount it will be reduced to one installment, otherwise the repayment will be spread over several weeks. To borrow of the family is less popular because the repayment normally has to be done quicker and at once. The moneylender has as advantage the possibility of installments. But on the other side the high interest rates (from 4 up to 10% a month) make him less popular.

The food consumption is probably the most important indicator of the economic situation of the laborers, but also the housing situation plays an important role. In general the shelter of most laborers is very poor. A substantial part (more than 40%) of the respondents is actually living at the building site, in sheds of leaves and twigs. In some other cases they are living in the buildings they are working on. One-third of the laborers is owner of a higher quality house (mud walls).

Individual characteristics

The strong growth of the economic activities and subsequent the population in Hosur can also be found in the ratio autochtone/allochtone. Only 22% of the unskilled laborers is born in Hosur. Most of the total group (71%) is born in the rural area. Almost all (84%) of them are from Dharmapuri. Out of these figures it becomes clear that indeed the development is a recent one (see table 6.10).

It becomes clear that more than half of the allochthones have come to Hosur the last year. Striking is also the great number of the male commuters compared with the number of female commuters. This is also an indication that the freedom of movement for women is less than for men.

---

[6] This figure is a result of the calculation of the mean food consumption per day per person. For 4 persons per day Rs 8 is needed for rice and Rs 3 for other ingredients. So per person Rs 2.75 is needed per day (price level of 1985). This figure is without the drinking water which (if it has to be bought) will cost Rs 1.4 - 2.1 per person per day (Barathan 1980).

Table 6.10 Period of living in Hosur

	male	female
commuters	17%	4%
autochtones	19%	24%
< 1 year	46%	40%
1 - 6 year	12%	22%
6 - 10 year	2%	2%
> 10 year	4%	8%

Source: own survey 1985.

The illiteracy of the population is high. Three quarter of them cannot read nor write. It is specially this group that is earmarked to unskilled work. The illiteracy of women is higher than of man (86% respectively 68%). It seems to be that the education of boys is still more important than the education of girls. Looking at the education level of the respondents it becomes clear that the situation of women is even worse than that of men (see table 6.11).

Table 6.11 Level of education

degree	male	female
1 - 2	20.8%	-
3 - 4	20,8%	50%
5 - 6	29,2%	50%
7 - 8	12.5%	-
9 - 10	8.3%	-
SSLC or more	8.3%	-

Source: own survey 1985.

It is striking that the level of education of a number of unskilled construction laborers is rather high. Except for this formal education a great number (64%) of the respondents has other skills, especially in the field of agriculture (82%). This also makes clear that most of the respondents have a rural background.

6.3.2 The labor-conditions of unskilled construction laborers

This paragraph will deal with the labor-conditions of unskilled construction laborers through the following subjects: regularity of work, wage situation, labor experience and labor organizations.

Regularity of work

According to Myrna Blake (n.d.) it is clear that construction is not a sector where labor contracts are normally used. None of the laborers possesses a labor contract. Therefore the employee depends on heavily the goodwill of the employer. On the other side most of the respondents (57%) are not afraid to lose their jobs, because 'it is easy to find another job'.
The work done by unskilled construction laborers consists most times of carrying activities. The loads that have to be carried weight approximately 15 to 20 kg. Rubbish, sand, water, stones and cement are the materials that are transported. Other activities consist of the breaking of stones in small pieces (a raw material for concrete), the sprinkling of water over just poured concrete to avoid cracks

in drying concrete, etc. The kind of unskilled work hardly differs between man and woman. But an important difference exists between the level of training of both sexes. In none of the cases women get a training and because of this they will never become a (semi-)skilled construction laborer. From the men more than one-quarter gets a training. Women do not get a training because most men think that women are not able to do skilled construction work. Further, women work often short periods or irregular in the construction sector, what is said to be a reason for getting less training.

The number of working weeks per year is connected with the sex (see table 6.12) and related to the traditionally different tasks of men and women. The women are expected to do the domestic work (in two-third of the cases their income is additional). The man is responsible for the earning of the household income. The most important reasons to work less than the maximum possible weeks are 'no work' (62%) and 'illness' (14%).
Most of the laborers (87%) work 8 hours per day, the rest works more (upto 12 hours).

Table 6.12 Number of weeks with work per year

weeks	male	female
52	26.9%	14.9%
48 - < 52	23.1%	4.3%
39 - < 48	23.1%	6.4%
26 - < 39	17.3%	27.6%
13 - < 26	3.9%	23.4%
< 13	5.8%	23.4%

Source: own survey 1985.

Wage situation

Despite the fact that men and women do almost the same work the payment of women is lower than of men. The mean income per day for man is Rs 12 and for women Rs 7 only. The general opinion of contractors is that women get less salary than men because men do their work faster, do work that is more heavy and are higher skilled. The level of payment appears not to be connected to the number of hours laborers are working daily. Some must work 10 hours for Rs 6, others 'only' 8 hours. Children normally get a few rupees less per day than adults.

Next to this basic payment a number of respondents (24%, of which three-quarter is women) get an allowance. This is an extra amount, paid for very heavy or additional work like 'concrete work', the finishing of some work in the evening, the guarding of the building site at night and also for being on time every day. The amount of the allowance varies from Rs 1 to 10 per day, but one should keep in mind that for instance concreting is very heavy work. The laborers are most of the times not able to work the next day because the cement grates the skin of their hands. Not everybody is considered for this kind of work that gives extra payment. In general the contractor has a fixed crew who is working a long time with him already. Next to the allowance in money some laborers get an allowance in kind (23%). Of course this depends again on the goodwill of the contractor.

Labor satisfaction

Though work in the construction sector is seen as very heavy, in general the laborers think positive about their work. The greatest part is satisfied with their payment, the number of labor hours as well as the job-security (respectively 65%, 76%, 77%). However there is a difference between men and women (see table 6.13).

Table 6.13 Satisfaction with the payment, labor hours and job-security

	male	female
payment	65%	64%
labor hours	85%	66%
job-security	94%	58%

Source: own survey 1985.

Specially in relation to the number of labor hours and job-security the men appear to have a more positive attitude than women. It seems that women think they lose their jobs more easily than men do. In fact women are more often (32%) threatened with dismissal than men (12%). The low satisfaction of women compared with men is caused by the fact that most female have a double task (domestic and construction). On average female construction laborers work daily 11.4 hours, of which 3.7 hours is needed for the domestic part of their task.

Labor organizations

In Hosur there are no unions or other labor organizations who are dealing with the labor-conditions of the unskilled construction laborers. There is a 'workers union', but this organization is not active in the construction sector. The negotiations on working conditions is done on individual basis. Because of this and the great number of unskilled laborers the negotiation position of the laborers is very weak. Since the laborers do not have a labor contract, the employers are able to fire them any minute they want to. Most of the laborers have the opinion that they will benefit from a labor organization. However, they do not have the time nor the knowledge to set up such an organization. Organizing the laborers seems to be a positive step in the right direction of improvement of their position. However, as long as they are willing to work under very bad conditions and as long as organizing seems to them to be a risk factor for getting fired, organizing of laborers as an expedient to improve their situation will be very laborious.

6.4 Conclusions

The growth pole policy of Hosur resulted in a strong rise of employment, mainly for skilled laborers. In the new factories, there was only place for a limited number of unskilled laborers. In the unorganized sector one can find a lot of short-term wage workers in unregistered small firms (mostly small workshops), who have no letter of appointment. For this group of workers there is no labor-legislation, unions are not available, the wages are low and the working hours long. In spite of the bad labor-conditions it is striking that these workers are fairly satisfied about their labor-security. It can be concluded that improvement of the labor-conditions of the permanent and registered short-term wage workers is mainly a political question: labor-legislation must be improved and executed! For unregistered short-term wage workers improvement may come from changes in the labor-relations, for instance by starting cooperations.

The population growth resulted in a growing amount of construction activities and as a consequence an attraction of a large number of unskilled laborers. The short-term effect of this development has been that many unemployed have found a new job, generating income for their households. Besides a number, in particular male workers, have been able to obtain a training and became semi-skilled. The surplus of construction laborers results in a selection of the workers; this is negative for women and older people.

Work in the construction sector is very heavy, but in general the laborers think positive about their work. In particular male laborers are satisfied with their payment, the number of labor hours as well as the job-security. The negotiation position of the construction laborers is still very weak. So far they do not have the time nor the knowledge to set up labor organizations.

7. The struggle for water: competition between industries and households

Joanne Heyink Leestemaker

The water problems of individual households are strongly determined by the development policy chosen by the state government. The growth of the industrial sector and the irrigated agriculture are subsidized by the state in order to develop the area. Investments have been made for the water-supply of the commercial sector and hardly for the local population.
The primary objective of this section is to quantify the link between the demand for and supply of water for domestic purposes. In order to get a clear picture of the water problems of Hosur, both the general demand and the supply structure have to be analyzed.

7.1 Changing demand for water in Hosur

The transformation of Hosur from a rural town into a growth pole affects the overall demand for water, as well as the composition of the demand. On the whole the shift in the pattern of water use can be characterized by the process of modernization with elements of irrigated agriculture, industrial use, and more domestic water consumption, because of population growth.

7.1.1 Domestic water demand

The domestic demand has increased rapidly, due to a more modern lifestyle and population growth. The changing pattern in domestic water consumption is found in the choice (and need) for different sources (private well, private tap and public sources, as handpumps, wells and taps) and the differentiation in the quantity. A well was the common source for water before 1970. In Hosur most households had access to a well near the house. In the eighties most wells in Hosur are still in use, new ones are being built. Unfortunately the water drawn from these wells is no longer safe and fresh enough for drinking purposes. The few fresh wells are in private ownership and carefully maintained by the owners. Inhabitants of Hosur without access to private tap water draw water for drinking and cooking purposes from public taps and handpumps. Easily available water (well, or surface water) is used for washing, cleaning etc.

Based on the survey (1988) the following figures were calculated with respect to sources with public access (public wells, handpumps and public taps): the average minimum demand of 5 liters water per capita per day (l/c/d) for drinking and cooking and 25 l/c/d cleaning water, that means in total 30 litre domestic water use per capita per day. Households with a private well near the house generally use more water, estimated at 60 l/c/d. In case of a private tap connection the average minimum use is 30-60 l/c/d increasing to 60-100 l/c/d in case of full water-supply with toilet flush and bathroom.

7.1.2 Agricultural demand for water

In 1974 15% of all cultivated land was irrigated in the Dharmapuri district, against the Tamil Nadu state average of 43% (Soil Survey, 1974). Paddy, sugarcane, bananas and cotton are cultivated on these lands. Series culture, dairy farming and sugar cane factories are the most important agro-industries of the Dharmapuri district. Recently, new irrigated fields have been used for market gardening; vegetables, grapes and flower cultivation. With governmental help the number of irrigated acres has been extended, unfortunately no actual figures of total irrigated land are available.
Dry farming is still the dominant type of cultivation in the Dharmapuri district. The crops are ragi, jowar, cumbu, horsgram, redgram and cow pea. Traditional gardening is done with mango trees, coconut, arecanut and tamarind.

Farmers and government try to catch up with the overall trend in Tamil Nadu, large water reservoirs are constructed, irrigation pumps are set up and especially around Hosur small farmers have found a source of income in horticulture. It can be expected that the expansion of rural activities will lead to a rapid increase in the (agricultural) demand for water in Hosur.

7.1.3 Industrial demand

Before 1977 the industrial demand for water in Hosur taluk was negligible. Between 1977 and 1985 the construction of new factories and houses demanded a fair amount of water coming from wells near the building sites. From the start the industrial area was stimulated and organized by the state government, the water demand of the factories was acknowledged. In 1977 the SIPCOT Water-Supply Scheme was founded to fulfil the demand for all factories. In 1988 the factories formulated a total demand of 3150 m^3 water per day, whereas the total domestic demand in 1988 is estimated at 2400 m^3 per day.

7.2 Changing supply of water in Hosur

7.2.1 Availability of water around Hosur

The Dharmapuri district is composed of a series of plains, valleys, plateaus and hills of varying heights ranging from 245 to 1450 meters (800 to 4750 feet). Hosur is located at 915 meters above sea-level, high enough to benefit from an atmosphere that is relatively cool. The district has a semi-arid, tropical climate. The maximum temperature ranges from 29-36°C, the minimum (night) temperatures from 17-23°C. The physical infrastructure of water can be described in terms of three interrelated elements: rainfall, surface water and groundwater.

Rainfall

Hosur taluk benefits both from the South-West monsoon (250-360 mm rainfall between June and September) and the North-East monsoon 200-300 mm in October and November). The average total rainfall per year is 787 mm in Hosur, with substantial variations between 558 and 1.133 mm in dry and wet years within one decade.

Surface water

The Ponnair river drains the Mysore plateau and crosses the Hosur-Krishnagiri road 17 kilometers from Hosur town. A second major river in the Mysore Plateau is Chinnar river which runs of a lower level and joins the Chauvery river. Several smaller flows drain the area during the monsoons and join the Ponniar, Pambar or the Kalar river. Furthermore there is a number of small lakes in Hosur taluk. Hosur-town has two shallow lakes, which dry up in summer time, and one artificial lake, the Rama Nayakkan Tank, built as a water reservoir for the castle of the muslim sultan Tippu in 1780. The water level in this tank is an important sign for the inhabitants of Hosur; when the tank dries up, Hosur has serious problems with the supply of water coming from shallow wells and handpumps. The reason is that lake water indirectly contributes to the ground water level. However the lakes are stagnant water reservoirs and they are heavily polluted. The water is used only for irrigation and for washing clothes, cleaning cars. The borders of the lakes serve as public lavatories.

Groundwater

To reach the groundwater level a well 20-40 feet deep has to be dug, dependent upon the soil conditions. Without modern techniques and machine power, well irrigation is not very profitable in the taluk. Until the seventies farmers mainly produced a rain-fed crop like ragi as staple food-grain, which is suitable for dry lands. Recently the ground water in Hosur has been pumped at rates that exceed replenishment, thus causing the water-table to fall. Heavy pumping for irrigation in Tamil Nadu and pumping for industrial use especially in Hosur taluk has resulted in a lowering of the water-table of 30-90 feet in a decade. This decline resulted in the change of water quality in Hosur; wells which provided fresh drinking water for decades, became salty last years (see figure 7.1).

7.2.2 Water-supply systems in Hosur

Dharmapuri district with its semi-arid climate and hard rocky soils has always experienced scarcity of water. Before the seventies agricultural and domestic water-supply was provided by human or animal power. In step wells the irrigation water was and is drawn by hand. In deeper wells the water for irrigation was drawn by a bullock and/or a man, walking in circles to turn the water wheel. In this way some old handmade tanks provided water for centuries.

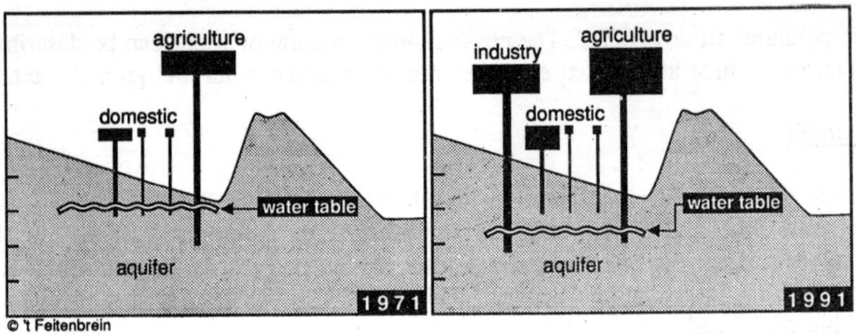

Figure 7.1 Effects of the falling water-table at domestic water-supply

The domestic wells for drinking water were dug and maintained by private house owners. Water was (and often is) drawn from the well by hand with a pulley and a rope. In temples and at market places there were wells for public use.
At the turn of this century the taluk had - in total - 1.286 wells which were built, maintained and used in a labor-intensive privately-owned distribution system. The constraints of this distribution system are land ownership, traditional knowledge and technology, man/animal power and the accessibility to groundwater. In combination with development planning and direct investment, modern technology and mechanical power have been applied since the seventies to uplift the backward district[1].

The newly built water schemes for irrigation and, particularly for industries, represent a capital-intensive distribution system. Dams, reservoirs, tube and infiltration wells, pumps, booster stations, pipe lines and water towers have provided modern water-supply systems. For these supplies human and animal power no longer provide a significant limitation. Capital, land ownership and scientific knowledge are the dominant factors in the modern water-supply. Tubewells for handpumps are on average 100 feet deep, a mechanical pump works often at 200 feet (Ganapathi 1988). With knowledge of the physical water infrastructure and heavy drills, pumps and pipe lines, water can be supplied in the driest area of Tamil Nadu. However, in the long run mining of ground water through excessive pumping can create serious groundwater drought in Tamil Nadu (Bandyopadhyay 1987).

In contemporary Hosur supply systems, based on human/animal power and mechanical power, operate parallel to each other. In some cases modern mechanical water pumps have replaced the wells. In times of energy scarcity (power cuts and fuel scarcity are regular phenomena) and when the new technology fails, people relapse into the traditional supply system.
Keeping this in mind the supply systems can be subdivided according to their power requirements into two groups. One based on human/animal energy (wells and handpumps with a depth of 20-100 feet) and the other on mechanical energy (mechanical pumps with a depth of 200 feet with an overhead tank, water tower and piped supply system with taps).

[1] The Tamil Nadu Water-Supply in cooperation with the Tamil Nadu Housing Board and for industry the SIPCOT Water-Supply Scheme and for agriculture the Kelavarapalli Reservoir Project.

Three different water-supply types can be distinguished: for respectively households, agriculture and industry. In the next paragraph the water-supply for these three types will be analyzed.

7.2.3 Supply structure for domestic water

The structure of the supply system in Hosur will be discussed in three clusters of neighborhoods (see figure 7.2).

I Housing schemes with modern water-supply system where around 30% of Hosur's population live.

II The old town and the unorganized new neighborhoods with its wells, pumps and taps, and 1200 private tap connections where 60% of Hosur's population live.

III Peripheral neighborhoods with wells and some pumps, which account for 10% of the population.

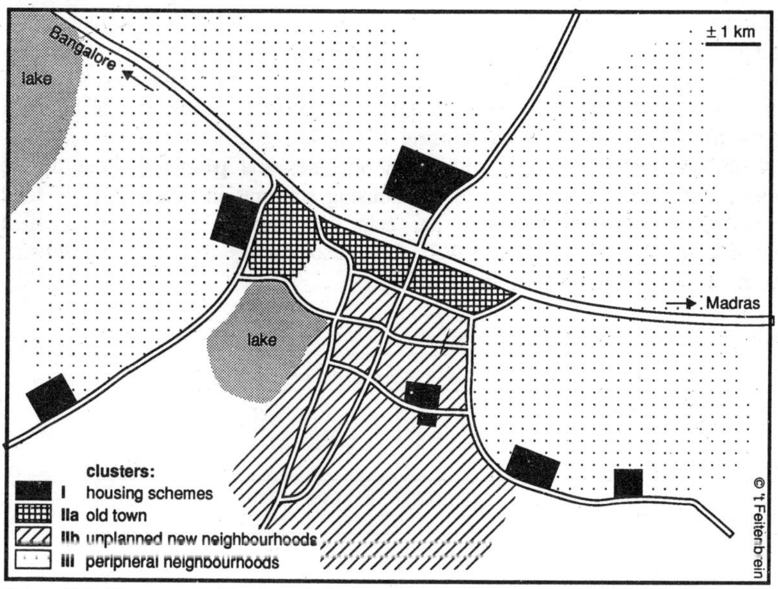

Figure 7.2 Hosur: neighborhood clusters I, II, III

I

In all housing schemes a piped water-supply system is in operation. The water-supply in these housing schemes has been collectively arranged by the Tamil Nadu Housing Board (TNHB). Water is pumped from deep borewells and stored in three TNHB-owned overhead tanks. From here water is distributed to the houses through a network of pipe lines. For the two large housing schemes water is pumped from a reservoir near Thally to Hosur. Other schemes are provided with water from borewells in the surroundings of Hosur.

Most flats have one tap connection and as a result of rationing water is supplied by the tap 15 to 30 minutes per day (per two days in the dry period). In some housing schemes the houses are provided with water tanks with a store capacity of 200-400 liters. In the smaller houses people store the tap water in plastic drums and pots.

Water taxes are 6 per cent of the house rent. This implies that a family in a small flat (Rs 275 per month rent) pays Rs 16.5 per month water tax, about half a rupee per day (1988 prices). In times of water and power scarcity the dwellers have to rely on the two or three handpumps which are still located in the housing schemes. When the taps do not provide any water the inhabitants use these handpumps and relapse further into the traditional water-supply network of the peripheral neighborhoods.

In the dry season when the demand for domestic water is really high, TVS-company and other large employers order lorries full of fresh water for their employees in the housing schemes.

Access to tap water

The housing schemes are built for employees in the industrial, governmental and banking sector. Access to the houses is given to households with a guaranteed, regular income in accordance with the income group for which the house was built. In this way around 14.000 people are provided with shelter and piped water for a part of the day. Table 7.1 gives an overview of the year of building and distribution of houses in the housing schemes.

It is obvious that households with lower incomes and people without formal employment hardly have access to the housing schemes in Hosur. Of the total number of houses not even one per cent has been built for the so-called Economically Weaker Section (EWS). This also implies that these households have no access to the modern water-supply.

Table 7.1 Number of newly built houses in the housing schemes

Income Group	1979-85	1986	1987-89	total	%
High (> 30.000 Rs/annum)	658	37	509	1204	32.2
Middle (15.000 - 30.000 Rs/annum)	403	131	779	1313	35.1
Low (8.401 - 15.000 Rs/annum)	260	481	447	1188	31.8
EWS (< 8.401 Rs/annum)	36			36	0.9
Total number of houses	1357	649	1735	3741	100.0
Average household size 3.8					

Source: Tamil Nadu Housing Board 1988.

II

The housing composition in the old town is mixed, there are streets with 50-100 year old houses and newly built blocks of flats. The unorganized new neighborhoods have a mixed structure of new one- and two-storied houses, mostly privately owned.

Between 1982 and 1988 the town panchayat of Hosur provided 1189 private tap connections mostly in the center of the town. Tap connections are only available in twenty streets of Hosur and in some of these streets bribes of Rs 2000 had to be paid before the Water Department was prepared to make the connection.

The network of these taps is supplied with water from the infiltration wells in the Ponniar river. From here the water is pumped through a 17 km pipe line over a slope of 100 meters into the main overhead tank in the middle of Hosur.

Next to the private taps, fifty public taps have been distributed in Hosur-town.

Because of rationing by town zone, water comes from the tap 15 to 30 minutes per day (per two or three days in the dry period). Taps at the end of the line are often without water all day. In the dry period of the year - from March to June - this water-supply system can provide only 25 per cent of the normal capacity. As an exception the Water Department ordered lorries with water for the population of Hosur-town in March 1986. However, this action was seen as an extreme case and will not recur according to the Water Department. It is hoped that a permanent solution will be found in a pipe line from the Kelavarapalli reservoir. This requires the agreement as well as funds from the state government.

The official costs for water is the fixed watertax of Rs 15 per month for a daily supply of 350 litre water free of charge (10.500 liter/month) and Rs 1 maintainance charge. Water costs total Rs 16/month. Extra water costs Rs 1.25 per 1000 litre.

In 1988 around 80 per cent of the inhabitants of cluster II had no access to the private water tap system of Hosur. The water-supply of around 24.000 people relies on 50 public taps, 43 handpumps and some dozens of wells. The network of wells was the traditional water source in Hosur. In the sixties the local government had dug seven large public wells for the supply in town, which are still in use. Between 1980 and 1988 the Water Department installed 43 handpumps spread out over the town.
In the last decades some of the richer houseowners have built their own wells or borewells for mechanical pumps. The costs of digging a well is related to the depth (20-30 feet) and varies between Rs 9500 and Rs 16000 (1988 prices). The price for a borewell (4.5 inch diameter, 200 feet depth) is Rs 9000. These prices show that only the upper class of Hosur can invest in a private source of water-supply.
An additional element is the quality of water-supply by different sources; the Ponniar water running from the taps is purified, however many shallow wells and handpumps give salty or insalubrious water which cannot be used for drinking and cooking purposes. Only deep tubewells, some handpumps and the mechanical pumps with a 100-200 feet depth give fresh water.

III
The peripheral neighborhoods are characterized by a rapid growth of the population. More and more people are building their own houses or renting a room in rental blocks built by a landlord. The location of the houses is often next to small villages in the surroundings of Hosur. Water-supply is a real problem in these neighborhoods. In general the landlords do not include water-supply in their package of services. In addition the Water Department of Hosur-town hardly provides these houses with a water source. Only four or five handpumps have been installed in the peripheral areas.

7.2.4 Supply structure for irrigation water

Irrigation sources are the rivers Ponniar, Pambar and tanks. Parallel to the traditional sources and types of supply of irrigation water, mechanical pumps are

used to pump ground water and distribute it over the fields. This is done mainly by private farmers. Credits and bank loans are used for investments in private supply systems. The water tax for farmers is counted per irrigated acre and crop. To protect the water-table in Hosur, the subcollector declared a ban on the private use of surface water of the lakes for irrigation in 1987.
The government had planned to start large-scale irrigation projects in the seventies. Due to the problems with acquisition of land the main project was suspended for five years. According to proposals, the Kelavarapalli reservoir across the Ponniar river will irrigate 8.000 acres of land and a reservoir across the Chinnar river will irrigate 850 acres of land in the future. The water tax will be Rs 20 per acre/crop.

7.2.5 Supply structure for industrial water

Since 1977 the Hosur industrial sector operates its own water-supply system. This SIPCOT Water-Supply Scheme consists of 32 deep wells and heavy pumps draw the water and push it into the nine water towers at the SIPCOT area. The water towers have each a capacity of 140.000 gallon. In 1988 the 102 factories which had joined the Sipcot Water-Supply Scheme, were supplied with a sufficient total amount of 700.000 (= 3150 cubic meter) per day.
Initially the SIPCOT Water-Supply Scheme planned to make use of a newly built water reservoir near Kevaranapalli, 30 kilometers north from Hosur. The building of the Kevaranapalli-dam started in 1977 and was planned mainly for irrigation purposes. For the future extra supply of water SIPCOT made arrangements for a pipe line from the reservoir to the industrial areas.

7.3 Labor as a bridge between demand and supply of domestic water

One can make a division in labor-intensive and capital-intensive water-supply systems. Based on a water-supply survey (1988) it is estimated that 60% of the households in Hosur supply their domestic water from a labor-intensive source. As a result of capital-intensive water-supply systems 40% has access to private tap connection.
In this section we look at the labor that is required to consume the water from different sources from the household perspective. In the actual domestic division of labor, unpaid labor of women and children narrow the gap between the demand of the household and the supply of water. The better off households, without tap water, can substitute this unpaid household labor by paid servants and water carriers. We try to answer the question how the time per household spent on water-supply relates to the time women can use productively.

7.3.1 Unpaid labor of housewives and children

In Hosur most women select different sources for drinking water and the remaining household water demand. The source with the best quality is selected for the supply of drinking water. The choice of the source for their other domestic water demand is determined by distance, time and energy costs. Analyzing the time spent on water-supply in the three clusters of neighborhoods (see figure 7.2) we draw the following picture.

I

In the housing schemes 90% of the households use the same source for their drinking water and their other domestic water demand. 74% of the households obtain their drinking water from private tap connection, 65% of the household use tap water for the rest of their domestic demands too. Because of rationing water flows once in one or two days. The time schedule of the supply of water is uncertain to the population. If the water is running, reservoirs have to be filled. Consequently in this cluster most time is spent on waiting until the water is running through the pipe line. In the housing schemes with a small private overhead tank on top of the blocks, four to six households share one overhead tank. Water scarcity makes it necessary for individual houscholds to claim their part of the daily supply and to store the water in smaller drums inside the house. For this reason a 'water-watch' must be at home. This duty is mainly performed by the person who takes care of the household. This is not necessarily a housewife, it can be a family member without full time obligations outside the house.

II

The water-supply pattern in the old city and the unorganized new neighborhoods gives a more complicated picture: 34% of the households use one source. However, only half of this group (17%) receive all their water from private tap connections, 13.5% rely on public taps and 3.5% receive their total water demand from wells or handpumps.

Because of bad water quality on the one hand and long distances, and queues on the other hand, 66% of the inhabitants decide to use different sources. For three or four pots of drinking water they make use of the time consuming public taps or handpumps. One trip takes 10 to 30 minutes. They have to walk to the source, wait in the queue, tap the water and bring it home. In total, they spend 20 to 40 minutes a day for drinking water only.

Table 7.2 Percentage of households spending 10 minutes or more for one trip (25 liter) Hosur (N=281 1988)

Neighborhood	Schemes	Old City	Unorg. Nbh	Periphery	Hosur
Time per trip > 10 minutes Water:					
drinking	14.8%	63.3%	49.5%	64.8%	48.7%
rest	8.2%	26.6%	43.8%	50.7%	34.2%
Different source used	10.0%	75.0%	57.3%	76.1%	55.7%

Source: own survey 1988.

The rest of the water is taken from less time consuming sources, often the well. It takes 5 minutes for half of the inhabitants, 10 or more minutes for 35% and 4% spend more than 30 minutes on one trip. The minimum needs of a household is on average 8 to 20 pots per day (120 - 300 liter). More than one hour per day is spent on this. For cluster II we can conclude that 66% of the households spend around two hours of heavy labor on a minimum supply. In the old city the water situation is worse than in the unorganized neighborhoods (see table 7.2). According to the traditional division of labor mainly women and their children fetch the water. In households without women, however, young men fetch the water or a water carrier is hired.

III
In the peripheral neighborhoods, water-supply is extremely labor-intensive for some inhabitants. 24% use only one source for drinking and other water. The rich (21%) can rely on private tap connection. Others use private wells. The main group have to fetch their water from whatever source is available. The time spent per trip may run to one hour. The water used inside the house is restricted to the absolute minimum.

To conclude this paragraph we can say that the labor demands for water-supply differs for neighborhood and choice of source. In cluster I water-supply is not so much energy but time consuming; somebody has to stay at home to collect the water running from the tap. In cluster II for the 66% without access to private taps, a limited water-supply demands two hours per day, often by women and children. In cluster III water is extremely labor-intensive for the majority of the people. Therefore the amount of water consumed is as small as possible.

7.3.2 Paid labor of water carriers

In times of water scarcity the professional group of water carriers in Hosur is expanding. The better off households with no free labor available make use of the services of a water carrier. In 1988 we counted roughly 150 professional water carriers in Hosur, divided into three subgroups. There is a group of about one hundred female water carriers. Like all women they carry each two water pots of 15 litre on their head and hip in one trip from the source to the house. For this labor they can earn Rs 0.25 per pot but most households pay a lower price for a daily supply of 6-10 pots, Rs 30-40 per month. This kind of job seems to be a residual from an old service system; like domestic servants the water carriers receive the daily leftovers from the client's kitchen and once a year they get a sari and clothes for their children.

The male water carriers with cycles form a smaller group of 15 professionals in Hosur. They provide water to households in six pots per turn hanging on their cycle. The earnings are the same as those of the female water carriers. A professional group by tradition are the water men with bullock carts. Around 45 men with carts bring water to large-scale consumers such as lodges, hospitals and rich households with store capacity. A drum of 180 litre is filled with water from a private well and carried to the customer by cart. The price they ask is Rs 3 to 4 per trip. In the dry season a higher price is asked (Bark 1989).

7.3.3 Opportunity costs of female labor

The labor saving capacity of piped water-supply has been limited in Hosur until now. In neighborhoods with piped water someone has to stay at home to collect water. An increase of time and labor demands for the domestic supply is observed in neighborhoods with labor-intensive supply systems. This as result of the conflicting demands and the decline of the water-table. And hence at town level the direct link between piped water and rising productivity of women in Hosur can be seriously questioned.

If we turn to the household level only in better off families the care for water can be taken by a grandmother or servants can be hired. Some women in this group have access to paid jobs, their monthly salary is Rs 275 to 1000 (1986 prices). An indication of the opportunity costs of their labor is Rs 2.4 to 3.3 per hour (see table 7.3). An argument can be made that these households pay Rs 16 per month water tax and do not have to spend 60 hours work on water-supply at an average price of Rs 2.85. In theory it means a profit of Rs 171-16=Rs 155 per month. So it is profitable to replace domestic water-supply for productive work.

Table 7.3 Working time and profit of female labor in Hosur

Time: Respondent	%/ day unpaid	%/ day paid	%/ day commuting	working time total	per hour profit
Supervisor	8	37	4	47%	2.4 Rs
Teacher	12	43	4	59%	3.3 Rs
Water carrier	14	43	-	57%	1.15 Rs
Street seller	6	58	4	68%	0.21 Rs

Source: own survey 1986.

On the other side of the spectrum we have the poorest women who have to work for the survival of their family. They have no access to piped water neither to formal paid employment. On the contrary they work many hours per day, but their profit per hour is low: Rs 0.21 to Rs 1.15 (average: Rs 0.68) for heavy work. On top of that they have to supply their own domestic water from a labor consuming source. Counting the opportunity costs of their labor in the same way the following is the outcome: 60 hours * Rs 0.68 = Rs 40.8 per month. If they should have piped water and they should pay the water tax the profit will still be on the side of the households: Rs 40.8 - Rs16 = Rs 24.8 per month. In the actual situation of Hosur these women lack the opportunity to save time on water-supply in an other way than cutting their water demands.
For the large group of women who are not involved in paid work the opportunity costs are difficult to calculate, for that reason we leave this group out of this analysis.

To sum up it can be argued that at household level on both sides of the spectrum of working women in Hosur it is profitable to have access to private tap water; although women with formal employment benefit economically much more than women working in informal jobs. Actually the first group is served by the government with piped water, the second group is not.
However, the opportunity costs of labor fail to indicate the potential rise in productivity. Next to the availability of time women need access to productive sectors of society.

7.4 Conclusions

From the above we can conclude that since 1977 government and panchayat have invested in Hosur taluk considerable manpower and money in the construction of a modern mechanical water-supply system for both domestic, agricultural and industrial use. Within ten, fifteen years, 40 per cent of the population of Hosur has been served with piped water and although the supply is exceeded by the demand, most of the agricultural demand and the total industrial demand are met.
Seen from the supply side the results are encouraging. However if we look at the distribution of the supply another picture begins to take shape.

We notice a division between the efforts made by the panchayat government and the state government. It is obvious that at local level limited funds and manpower are available for operating a water-supply system in the town. More than half the population rely on public sources for their water-supply. In fact they rely on the efforts of the local authorities. The wells and handpumps installed by the town panchayat are labor-intensive in their supply system. Due to their scarcity and the rationing of the water the fifty public taps are also labor- and time-intensive.
In addition to this through overpumping the water-table is falling. Due to this, water from some sources with a depth of 20 to 100 feet became salty and unsafe for drinking.
We must conclude that a combination of falling water-tables and increasing demand makes the supply inadequate for 60 per cent of the population.
The state government supports the large-scale capital-intensive water-supply projects. Specific groups in society benefit from the outcome of these projects. We saw that only the formally employed with regular incomes over Rs 8.400 per year had access to the housing schemes with piped water. Furthermore the industrial sector and the landowners profit from the state efforts. Consequently the modern sector of society - in agriculture, industry and housing schemes - is exploiting water from deeper levels at the expense of the people without any entitlement in the modern sector. The rich can overcome the falling water-table by using more powerful machines and longer pipe lines. The poorer section of society is unable to do this and the panchayat is hardly in the position to help them.

The labor requirements for water-supply are low in the neighborhoods where some women have access to the formal labor market. At an average profit of Rs 155 per month they can replace domestic water-supply for productive work. If the house is not supplied with piped water by the local government, it is more costly: a water carrier has to be hired for Rs 30 to 40 a month (Rs 14-24 more for less quantity of water with bad quality). Women with paid work in the informal sector can not afford a water carrier, but they would profit from private tap water for Rs 16 water tax. In addition to the savings in labor and energy, the health of the family can improved by tap water. This can be a major time saving effect for the women living in the town.

8. HUNTING FOR WASTE: THE FRINGE OF THE GROWTH POLE

Nico Kerkum

In most third world countries people can be found who are making a living out of collecting waste materials. Ragpickers are mainly specialized in collecting household-garbage: this contains a great number of materials that can be separated difficultly. The collecting, separating and processing of the garbage is less interesting for the big recycling factories because the work is very labor-intensive. This makes it the niche of the marginal groups like the ragpickers. Industrial waste on the contrary is sold directly to middlemen without the intervention of the ragpickers.

8.1 Recycling and ragpickers

The ragpicker is part of a hierarchical 'recycling network', where also other actors play their role: middlemen and factories of different sizes. The literature on contemporary urban waste collectors is relatively sparse and case-studies are few and scattered (Birkbeck 1979, Furedy 1989).
Recycling of waste takes place automatically when a shortage of raw materials appears or when the prices of waste and/or the energy needed to change them into raw materials are lower than the prices for raw materials on the commercial market. One can find the ragpickers at the bottom of the recycling network. They never sell their items directly to factories that are using waste materials as an input; always middlemen play an intermediate role.

The composition of the waste available to the ragpickers is not very rich of valuable materials due to the fact that in a poverty economy only things are thrown away which have no immediate value[1]. Another reason is that the most valuable parts of the waste (scrap and bottles) are often picked out by the scavengers and servants before dumping.
The emphasis of this study is directed to: the way in which the ragpickers are collecting the materials, their bargaining position at the buyer, their social and economic characteristics, and the constraints they are facing every day.

[1] Furedy (1984) refers to the waste of Calcutta as the cleanest waste, all useful things have been removed already.

8.1.1 Ragpickers in Hosur

Most of the migrants to Hosur have been attracted by the employment opportunities at SIPCOT-area. They have come mainly from cities like Madras, Bangalore and other (second order) towns in Tamil Nadu.[2] But apart from these better off people, also poor people from the surrounding areas came to Hosur in search for jobs. Due to their low level of education (if any) there are not many jobs in the industrial area for them. They have to make their living in the traditional, informal economy of Hosur. Some of them are successful, but a growing part are not. Amongst the latter group one can find people who earn their living with 'ragpicking'[3]. One of the consequences of the growth pole policy has been the attraction of poor people to 'promising' Hosur, who were not able to find work and can only make a little money out of ragpicking.

It was very difficult to find and contact the ragpickers in Hosur. The nature of the ragpicking, which is considered as impure in the caste-society of India, gave specific caste-based problems in contacting them. The first ragpickers approached were very suspicious and it was nearly impossible to start further contact. The local scavengers, however, had a close relationship with children, who were collecting waste on the garbagedump every day[4]. By using these key informants it was possible to contact 25 ragpicker families of which 42 people were engaged in ragpicking.

8.1.2 Ragpicker families

It appeared to be very difficult to get a clear picture about the number of ragpickers in Hosur. From various local informants and from own observations the total number of ragpickers is estimated to be between 160 and 200. This estimation seems realistic since there are about 50,000 ragpickers out of a population of 5 million in Madras (Kalpagam 1983).

The ragpicking families are mainly concentrated in the eastern outskirts of Hosur, an area officially named Therpetai (see map 4, chapter 4). Therpetai is dominated by a huge hill on which a temple is built. It is enclosed between the roads to Krishnagiri and Rayakotta and situated just beside the burial and cremation place of Hosur. The area is divided in a low lying legal part and a

[2] See chapter 3.

[3] In this paragraph the terms ragpicker and ragpicking are used to refer to people collecting waste materials and the activity itself because these are the most common terms in India. The term scavengers is for instance widely used in Latin America but in India it indicates the dustmen paid by the municipality. Ragpicking can be defined as a activity involved in the collection of waste materials, done directly for subsistence.

[4] The bullock-carts with which the scavengers are collecting the garbage were emptied three times a day on the garbagedump. At those times children were waiting for the carts to come, to take out whatever was useful to them. The rest of the day they are collecting in the streets of Hosur itself. Only a few adults (mainly women coming from Bangalore) were seen on the garbagedump regularly.

illegal high part which the dwellers have named Parvathi Nagar. Approximately one-quarter of Parvathi Nagar is still untilled due to the sometimes abrupt slopes and enormous rocks through which it is almost impossible to build a hut. Most ragpickers are living in Parvathi Nagar. The huts are mostly of a very poor quality, some of the ragpickers do not even have a house and live under the rocks. In Therpetai, according to data gathered in 1985, totally around 1000 households are living there (with an average householdsize of 5.3). According to the dwellers (there are no data on Parvathi Nagar at the Town Panchayat) most of the houses were built during the last 10 years. There are no amenities at all in the higher area of Parvathi Nagar; Therpetai has three waterpumps and electricity is provided to the shops and some houses along the main roads. The water problems are huge in the area: a few pumps for more than 5300 people. This part of Hosur is still growing fast.

Nearly all ragpickers migrated to Hosur. They were not able to find a job and had to take up ragpicking.

> *"I came to Hosur nine years ago hoping to find a job to sustain my family. I had a piece of land in a small village near Denkanikotta which I inherited from my father. This plot was already property of the family as long as I know. Unfortunately I didn't have the papers that proved that the land was mine and it was taken from me by a big farmer who registered the land under his name. We were evicted from our own land. In that time I had heard from family that I would be able to find a job in Hosur, but when I came here there wasn't a proper job for me. After having worked as a coolie, which I couldn't keep up because I couldn't work every day, I started ragpicking. A friend learned me the trade and although I don't like the work at all I was at least able to make a living".*

Almost all ragpicker families contacted, had severe medical problems[5]. Besides that there are also severe alcoholproblems in most households, the majority of the men is drinking one bottle of toddy or arrack a day. The money spend on alcohol is a serious problem for the rest of the family, not only because a large part of the householdincome is spent on it but also because the wives and children are often beaten. Most households appeared to be incomplete because one of the parents died or abandoned the household.

> *Raja's mother:*
> *"My husband couldn't cope with the situation and started to drink more and more. He took every penny Raja and I were making and we were hungry and I was beaten often; even the children couldn't escape from his anger. Finally he left with another woman from Hosur. I don't miss*

[5] In every family approached, one or more members of the houschold were more or less ill or handicapped. The rates of infant mortality are very high. Skindiseases were most common due to the nature of their work. Diseases of the lungs (amongst others tuberculoses) were widespread among the ragpickers probably caused by the bad foodquality and hygienic conditions. Some men were suffering of livertroubles due to the heavy drinking.

him at all because now the children and I aren't beaten any more and the children have at least one proper meal a day".

Out of in total 42 ragpickers about 40% is below the age of 16 (24% below 10). All appeared to be of backward castes (e.g. Harijan) or scheduled tribes. The majority is illiterate, had no education at all and the parents do not send their children to school. The daily income is in 60% of the cases below Rs 10, 32% said to earn between Rs 10 and 20 per day (8% earns more). The average total household income is Rs 140 per week, the variation is shown in the next table.[6]

Table 8.1 Average total household income per week

income (Rs)	number	%
upto 100	9	38.5
100 - 200	12	50.0
200 and more	3	11.5
Total	24	100.0

Source: own survey 1986.

Not all households are completely dependent on the money earned with ragpicking, but in half of the families the ragpickers income forms more than 75% of the total household income. The social characteristics are summarized in table 8.2. The figures presented about the debts are not completely reliable[7].

The ragpickers are socially isolated which manifests itself in the absence of contacts with people in Hosur other than relatives or people from the same caste. This is due to the kind of work ragpickers are doing, which is regarded as inferior[8] in the Hindu society.

A consequence of this isolation is their difficulty (or absence) to have contacts with governmental institutions (their illiteracy also plays a role). All things for which it is needed to approach the government are not available for ragpickers. They have for instance no rationcard, a facility provided by the government of Tamil Nadu to get discount on rice, sugar etc.

[6] Reliable income figures are always difficult to obtain and to check. Some daily incomes could be checked by staying with the respondent the whole day. Another way of checking appeared to be the gathering of the daily expenses of two families during two weeks. Data given by those respondents appeared to be corresponding with the earlier provided income-data.

[7] Many respondents told me that they were ashamed having debts. The figure is therefore, also because it was impossible to check, not completely reliable and I consider it as a estimation which is too high.

[8] Most literature is referring to ragpicking as inferior. See for instance: Kalpagam (1983), El-Hakim (1977), Blincow (1986), Garella (1985), Eekhout (1981) and Mukerjee (1975).

Table 8.2 Social characteristics of the ragpickers in Hosur.

	percentage
Sex of ragpickers	
% Male	45.0
% Female	55.0
Age distribution	
-15 years	37.7
16-30 years	31.1
31-45 years	20.0
45+ years	11.1
Residence	
Own house	25.0
Rented house	50.0
Nothing	21.4
Others	3.5
Place of origin	
Hosur	10.7
Dharmapuri district	57.1
Outside Dharmapuri district	21.4
Unknown	10.7
Marital status	
Married	44.4
Widowed	4.4
Single	51.1
Length of time in job	
-3 years	28.6
4-6 years	21.4
7-9 years	7.1
10+ years	25.0
unknown	17.8
Debts (Rs)	
- 500	32.1
501-1000	10.7
1001-2000	7.1
2001 and more	10.7
no debts	39.4

Source: own survey 1986.

8.2 Collecting and exchange

Some different ways of waste collecting can be distinguished. The ragpickers bring their materials to a buyer and after separating the waste the middleman buys their materials. In his turn the middleman sells the selected garbage to factories.

8.2.1 Different types of ragpicking activity

The ragpickers in Hosur can be divided into five groups distinguished according to the type of activity.

1. Ragpickers, mainly children and women, who are collecting their materials in the streets and the garbagedump.
2. People who collect their materials in the surrounding villages of Hosur, mostly going by bicycle.
3. Ragpickers who are collecting their materials in the sewerages in the neighborhood of jewelleryshops and sweep the dust in front of these shops.
4. Ragpickers, who are coming from Bangalore, collecting bone.

5. People who are buying the materials in Hosur, going from house to house.

Ad 1.
The 'street-ragpickers' are the poorest group of ragpickers with an average income of Rs 5 - 6 per day. Approximately 50 to 60 children and 20 women are collecting their materials in the streets of Hosur. Two women and 8 to 10 children can be found at the garbagedump regularly, at times the scavengers are emptying their bullock-carts. They collect everything that can be found and sold, but plastic (milkbags), scrap, cardboard and glass (pieces and bottles) are the main items.[9]

This group is the most vulnerable one, partly because only women and children are engaged in this line of work but mainly because their bargaining position at the buyer is very weak. As they bring in small quantities every day, they can be cheated more easily and they are less important for the buyer.

> *"The work is terribly heavy and I earn just enough to feed my children", told Lokhi. "I walk long distances with my baby on the arm and at the end of the day I'm exhausted. Fortunately my other children help me and they are hardly a nuisance. After collecting I have to go to the buyer to sort out the materials because he doesn't buy unsorted ones. He is often making troubles, the materials are too wet or dirty, he is always complaining. He subtracts some weight because the materials are wet or dirty[10]. All women and children who are collecting in Hosur and at the garbagedump have difficulties with this man but everyone keeps quiet out of the fear that he won't buy their materials any more[11]. Seldom I get a loan when I ask him and I've never got the sari he's providing for other ragpickers every year".*

In general it is more difficult for this group to get loans from the buyer than it is for other groups. So often they have to lend money from the moneylenders who are calculating huge interest-rates. They start working at 6-7 am and end the job at 4-5 pm, although some women work more than 12-13 hours a day.

Ad 2.
The largest group of ragpickers are those who go to the surrounding villages of Hosur to collect their materials. Approximately 70 - 100 men (it is exceptional that women are doing this) are engaged in this line of business. The variation in income is higher in this group than amongst the street-ragpickers but on the average the income is higher (Rs 12-13 per day). Sometimes they buy the

[9] All groups are also collecting the shells of coconuts and pieces of wood they find, which are used as fuel. Another material that is collected by the women is the dung of the cows which they dry in the sun and also use as fuel.

[10] This is a serious problem for this group. Especially in the rainingseason it decreases their income considerably.

[11] Although most ragpickers toid to have a good opinion about the buyer some ragpickers are full of criticism.

materials but when children are around the materials are exchanged for sweets. Another possibility is selling pots and buckets and trading in the old and broken ones. With the bicycle, that is rented in 80% of the cases, they peddle around 12 - 16 km per day. Recently more than 20 new 'cycle-ragpickers' have joined; the increasing competition decreases the income and increases the working hours (almost always more than 10 hours). The bargaining position at the buyer is better than that of the first group due to the fact that they bring in more materials of a better quality. The main items that are collected are plastic (the finest quality), scrap and precious metals like copper, brass and sometimes silver. Notebooks and magazines are also collected. Almost all 'cycle-ragpickers' are in debt with the buyer (sometimes upto Rs 2000).

Ad 3.
Some people (5-9) go to the jewelleryshops in the main streets of Hosur early in the morning. There they filter the sewerage water and collect the more heavy particles. They also sweep the dust in front of the shop, collect it and remove all the fine dust. At home they extract gold out of the collected material. On average they make Rs 15 per day. Sometimes the dust in the shop itself is collected by the jeweller and sold to the ragpickers. The people engaged in this kind of collecting are mostly having a bad health due to the mercury-gasses that escape during the extraction process. All children had burns (scars) due to playing with the acid used in the process.

Ad 4.
Another group of ragpickers (8-10) working in Hosur are people coming from Bangalore mainly to collect bone. Bone is not collected by ragpickers living in Hosur because it cannot be sold to the buyer. The reasons for this are firstly religious (the buyer in Hosur is Hindu) and secondly the nature of the material. It has to be stored for a rather long time and bone is starting to smell then. They come to Hosur as a consequence of the severe competition amongst ragpickers in Bangalore. The entry to the ragpicking is free in Hosur on contrary to Bangalore where even certain streetblocks are allotted to individual ragpickers.
They stay at friends or sleep near the railway station of Hosur. Often they work for one or two days in Hosur and then go to the other surrounding villages and towns to collect.

Ad 5.
The last group (5-8 persons) which is engaged in the waste material business are not really ragpickers but small merchants; buying materials from house to house and selling it to the buyer. Because of the nature of their activities and their considerable daily income (on average Rs 40 - 50) not much attention has been given to this group. However their real income is lower due to the fact that they do not work every day. The money needed for their trade is always borrowed from the middleman.

8.2.2 The middleman

Around twelve years ago the buyer came to Hosur from Madurai with a small sum of money. He started buying up waste materials from the ragpickers. He bought a piece of land in Therpetai and started his agency. He started to gain clients in a very smart way[12].

First of all he promised every ragpicker, who was willing to bring his or her materials every day, a free pair of clothes every year; a man gets a blouse and trouser, a women a sari. Secondly loans were given to all (starting) ragpickers who were willing to sell their materials to him exclusively. Those loans were given when a ragpicker needed the money because his pickings of the day were not enough to feed his family, or when money was needed for festivals, marriages or burials. The loans are free of interest and ought to be paid back when the ragpickers are able to, but usually their daily income is cut with one to four rupees. In this way the buyer was able to take over all clients of another middleman (established rather far away from Therpetai), who was buying waste materials from ragpickers too. This other buyer was not giving the benefits like the present buyer was doing and finally stopped competing with him. He started to give lower prices for waste materials from ragpickers and began buying waste from small workshops. Almost no ragpicker is selling his materials to him, so the Therpetai buyer has more or less the monopoly in Hosur at the moment. The buyer has a lot of influence in the ragpicker-community. He is providing not only loans and the once a year cloth but he also started to buy houses in Therpetai from ragpickers who were not able to pay back the loan they had with the buyer. He rented those houses to ragpickers who were bringing high quality materials every day and who were influential in the ragpicker-community. He keeps the rent low for these people and in exchange those renters keep the buyer informed of everything that is going on in the ragpicker-community. In this way the buyer is able to control the ragpickers in a very cunning way. The opinion of the ragpickers about this man is in general a good one. They see him as a 'philanthropist'.

> *"My daughter was getting married and I didn't had the money. I went to the buyer who gave me the Rs 1000. Now I'm paying him four rupees a day when it is possible. When I have a bad day, I don't have to pay".*
>
> *"I was really having troubles in getting enough materials this winter. I was sick for already a very long time and I couldn't buy enough rice for the children. He lent me the money when I asked him, without his help I would have starved".*

The buyer made and makes the ragpickers dependent of him and a patron-client relation has emerged[13]. The loans are 'free of interest' but the reality is

[12] All information considering the buyer has been obtained from former employees of this man and another middleman. The buyer himself was unwilling to give any information about himself or his business.

[13] A. Aziz (1984, p. 113) is referring to the patron-client relation as:
"There, however, has developed a system of buyer-seller tie-up and this has worked against the interest of the sellers in so far as it has resulted in some abusive practices like free service to the creditor, lower prices and overweightment."

different. Many ragpickers are in debt with this man, sometimes up to Rs 2500[14].

When Rs 4 or less is paid every day and Rs 500 is borrowed, it will take at least 125 days to pay off the loan, which mostly will take more time due to the inconstant availability of the materials. The loans are verbal agreements (only the buyer is doing recording it on paper) and the ragpickers trust him blindly. No one is able to remember how many instalments he/she has paid already and the buyer is making use of that and charges them even when the loan has been paid already. In this way the buyer gets a 'hidden' interest and makes the people believe that he is lending the money without interest. Since he is more or less having the monopoly in Hosur, he is making distinction amongst the individual ragpickers considering the earlier mentioned benefits and prices. The people who bring in the best quality materials and large quantities are getting better prices[15] and treatment from the buyer. The buyer is denying the for him less interesting ragpickers. E.g. he does not give once a year cloth or the loans and he gives lower rates for the offered materials and he is even sometimes refusing to buy up their materials. The latter happens when such a ragpicker is troublesome for him. Divide and rule has become his motto and he is having total control of the community.

Kalpagam (1983) recognizes the dependency of the ragpickers: she states that ragpickers seem to be independently self-employed[16] but the ragpicker is dependent on the capitalistic, industrialized sector of the economy as well considering the supply as the salespotential of the waste. Secondly there is the dependence relation with the buyer which is in fact also a coping mechanism. The buyer provides loans and supports the picker in difficult times in exchange for the promise to sell their materials exclusively to him. It is an agreement with mutual trust and both parties consider the agreement as fair, reasonable and justified. In this way the buyer becomes a kind of 'godfather'. This is a system created by the picker, in full awareness to cope with daily life and to assure their survival.

Breman (1976) remarks more in general:

> "The poor try to increase their security within the urban by entering into dependency relations with social superiors; in doing so they accept a wide range of contractual and semi-contractual commitments".

---

[14] The usual maximum that can be borrowed from the buyer is around Rs 500, but many exceptions are made.

[15] The prices of the waste are determined by the market (supply and demand) and by the middleman. The income of the ragpicker is, besides the latter, determined by his individual ability and working hours and quality of the material he/she is able to collect.

[16] More about the classposition of ragpickers in "Een tip van de sluier; een onderzoek naar het dagelijks leven van vuilrapers in Hosur, Zuid-India. N.M. Kerkum, 1990.

Beside cheating the ragpickers with the loans the middleman is also cheating them with the weight. Most ragpickers do not know how a balance is working so it becomes very easy to cheat. He also uses weights that have a lower weight than is indicated.
The prices given for the materials are not fixed, they vary regularly. Whether this was due to marketprices I could not make out but it can be another way to cheat the pickers. That the buyer is far from a philanthropist will be clear by now and the data from table 8.3 show that he must earn quite a lot of money.

Table 8.3 Prices and quantities of garbage materials

	costprice Rs	selling price Rs	quantity per month
magazines	1.00/kg	2.50	1/4 ton
notebooks	2.50/kg	4.00	
plastic	6.00/kg	9.00	2 ton
cardboard	1.00/kg	2.00	1/4 ton
scrap	1.10/kg	1.60	15 ton
3/4 bottles	0.90/bottle	1.20	200 sacks
1/4 bottles	0.30/bottle	0.50	
glasspieces	0.20/kg	0.35	12 ton

Source: own survey 1986.

The quantity indicated in table 8.3 for scrap, glasspieces and plastic (this concerns only the high quality plastic) make already an income of Rs 14,300 month. Whether this is correct could not be checked but from different sides people assured the researcher that he made at least Rs 8000 month.

These are the highest prices given by the buyer and is only given to regular 'customers' and ragpickers who bring large quantities. Only sorted materials are bought and after collecting the ragpickers sort out their materials which can take up to one and half hour. Another material that cannot be sold to the buyer, besides bone, is newspaper. The main reason is that old newspapers are used as a packingmaterial in shops and the people of Hosur themselves sell the old newspapers to the stores. Notebooks and magazines are only bought in large quantities (>100 kg). For cardboard only one price is given while there exist three kinds of quality.

The ragpickers do not store their materials but sell directly after collecting. Lack of storage space and the immediate daily need of the money earned with picking, certainly increases the middle man's profit. All bought materials are sold in Bangalore to other middlemen, who have specialized according the nature of the materials. In Bangalore a whole hierarchical network exists, build up in a similar way as Birkbeck (1979) describes for Cali[17].

---

17 See also A.Aziz (1984): Urban poor and Urban informal sector.

8.3 Conclusions

Because of the monopoly of the buyer in Hosur, he has an almost complete control of the ragpicker-community which is disadvantageous for the ragpickers because of the absence of other competitors. The cheating of the buyer is estimated to decrease the income of the average ragpicker with 10 to 20%.
The number of ragpickers is growing fast; this increases the competition and as a result the workinghours because the availability of the materials will become less. Compared to Bangalore it is much easier to become a ragpicker. The entry is free and no places are reserved by individual ragpickers.

From the figures of table 8.2 we can conclude that the ragpicking is a hard way to make a living. It is dirty, heavy and unhealthy work which puts a great strain on the physical condition of the ragpickers. The fact that more than 60% of the respondents is below the age of 16 is pointing to the fact that many children have to take up ragpicking early to contribute to the householdincome. The illiteracy rate amongst the ragpickers is more than 90% and there is no additional money for schooling available. More than 60% is in debt and in half of the approached families the income generated from ragpicking forms more than 75% of the householdincome, which marks the low income of the ragpickers. More than 20% of the respondents were not having any shelter at all and were sleeping on the streets or under the rocks. More than 75% of the respondents migrated to Hosur.

The drinking of the men, the diseases and other problems within the households, and the dependence on the moneyloans needed to meet their contingent expenses make life harder than it is already, especially for the women and children. The respondents were in general not aware of further processes of waste recycling beyond that of the buyer.

Birkbeck considers ragpicking as a refugee-job but in Hosur it became clear that ragpicking is an activity needed to survive. Although Birkbeck sees a self-esteem and recorded ragpickers feelings to be in control of their own lives I did not encounter one ragpicker who had that feeling.

From the research results an overview of the structural problems of the ragpickers in Hosur. Their main problems could be summarized as follows:

1. Like many others, their main problem is financial, on one hand caused by the nature of the work on the other hand the difficult financial situation is worsened by the practices of the buyer.
2. The lack of education which is in fact the most fundamental one. Only two families are sending their children to school.
3. The isolation of the ragpicker-community which manifests itself in the absence of contacts with the people of Hosur others than relatives or people from the same caste and the lack of constructive contacts with the local authorities.

It is likely, considering the number of ragpickers, that ragpickers contribute in a large extent to the cleaning of the streets and the recycling of waste materials.[18] Ragpickers are ignored by the local government[19] and can be regarded as the drawback of the growth pole policy. Only the more well-to-do people, who are employed in the industries, benefited from the government policy. In this way the government policy did increase the inequalities within Hosur[20].

[18] A.Aziz (1984, p. 137): "........, in the absence of waste collectors collecting this material, it would have literally gone waste having found no alternative use".

[19] Veena Garella (1985, .p 165): "The real value of the output is difficult to estimate. The service performed by pickers in disposing an estimated 40% of the solid waste of urban areas is neither recognized nor acknowledged by civic authorities".

[20] Steps have been undertaken to improve the present situation for the ragpickers in Hosur. In 1986 a project proposal based on the fieldwork results was written and submitted to ICCO, a non-governmental organization in the Netherlands. ICCO decided to finance the project, which started in july 1988. At the moment 60 ragpicker-children are attending the project-school regularly and adult-education has been started.

9. Factories and Families: Summary and Conclusions

Evert Meijer and Ko Heins

It would be an error to argue that the case study of Hosur provides anything but an intuitive insight into the role of a small town in the development process, but it does raise questions concerning the validity of policies that attempt to increase populations in the lower order centers to balance the urban hierarchy or to stimulate backward areas and inject activities and services which will spread into surrounding rural areas. In the long run it does often seem that planning policy, which attempts to diversify and broaden the economic base of small towns to spread these supposed economic benefits of the policy into the countryside, is wasteful.

In this book we touched on two central questions for evaluating growth pole policy:

a. what is the development potential of recently created new small-scale activities?
b. what is the position and what are the prospects of underprivileged and vulnerable groups in local society?

Hosur is located on the main road that connects Bangalore and Madras. It is situated quite near to the border with Karnataka at a distance of only 45 km from Bangalore, which is the fifth city of India with more than 4 million inhabitants. To most entrepreneurs in Hosur, particularly the larger ones, Hosur's closeness to Bangalore has been a distinct attraction. It gives them easy access to city accommodation, schools and hospitals, banking, travel and communication facilities. Equally important has been the access Bangalore provides for recruiting skilled manpower. To these pull factors are also added, to some extent, the push factor of the overgrowth of Bangalore and a consequent movement of industries to outlying areas. In the eighties the government of Karnataka has set up an industrial estate at Bommasandra, 20 km from Hosur, as a counter attraction to Hosur. Hosur is thus not so much in the heart of a backward area as it is proximous to a large metropolitan and industrial center. It is obvious that it has been this factor - which would ensure the success of an industrial estate scheme - that underlies the choice of Hosur on the part of the state government rather than any of the other urban centers in Dharmapuri for the programme of industrial development. It is hardly to be expected that such a center as Hosur, located at one edge of the backward region is likely to bring development for the whole district.

Therefore it can be concluded that the implementation of the development scheme itself in Hosur has been effected on the basis of one criterium - proximity to an industrial center - which does not have any place in the identification criteria for backwardness of peripheral regions.

9.1 Big factories and small workshops

The provision of physical facilities and financial incentives has resulted in not just a trickle of investment, but in an avalanche, considering the time period involved. The investment that has flowed is dominated by large companies and industrial houses of the state. This is clearly due to the nature of the schemes themselves, insofar as these give a strong impetus to large investors. The technology in use in the factories of medium and large size has been capital-intensive and demanding of a skilled labor force. The small units, on the other hand, have been characterized by a lower capital-intensity and have also absorbed more of the local, relatively unskilled labor force. There is little use of available local inputs by the industries. The absorption of the local labor in the factories has not been insignificant, but these generally find themselves in the low paid categories. The overall wage level itself is low, with levels in the small units being below those in the medium and large ones. One part of the strategy, that of providing for the social needs of the population, has not been taken as seriously as the other parts. Finally, managements in general have decided to retain wages at fairly low levels. The trickle-down effect of the subsidies is thus not likely to be very strong, at least in the short run.

The manner in which industrialization has been undertaken in Hosur - with emphasis placed on encouraging large-scale, capital-intensive industries; with the development of small-scale production producing ancillaries to the large ones; with a basis in investment invited from outside the area; without any product linkage with the backward area, and offering only low-paid, unskilled employment to the local population; and above all located on the periphery of the backward region - has had the net effect of subsiding the investment decisions of a relatively small group of major industrial concerns and little else.

In the Hosur-case it may be concluded that the industrial development policy has been highly successful. Several of the leading industrial houses in (South-)India have set up medium and large plants at Hosur, and some have stimulated small-scale satellite units as well. While the industrial houses dominate the medium and large units, and thus the overall investment in the area, the small units present a contrast. These units are sometimes set up by local entrepreneurs who would not have gone in for any investment at all, if it had not been for the concessions offered to the entrepreneurs in Hosur by the government. The

financial schemes would thus appear to have not only played a role in transferring investment that might otherwise have gone elsewhere, but also in calling out altogether fresh investment.
The small units at Hosur and the medium and large units are strongly differentiated by the technologies used. The technology mix, particularly in the medium and large units, is quite demanding of highly skilled labor. The small-scale enterprises, however, create employment with far less investment. It might be argued that the government incentives could have created more employment if they had been directed more at small-scale enterprises. Still, it is clear that since the larger-scale industrial sector is the principal client for the small-scale industrial sector in Hosur, the presence of larger-scale units in the present structure is inevitable.
Most of the employment that has been created as a result of the growth of the industrial units and the consequent increase in population has been in the commercial and services establishments that have come up. The number of shops, hotels, motor and auto works has risen considerably since the start of the industrial policy. Of course also the construction industry benefited from the booming industrial sector.

9.1.1 The role of small-scale industries

There has been extensive growth in the volume of production and employment in the large and small-scale sector in the past ten years. The growth can be attributed to the establishment of larger-scale enterprises in the industrial estates outside the traditional Hosur-town. There is a trickle-down effect to small-scale industrial units in Hosur. Growth mainly comes from the increasing number of units in this sector, while growth within existing units is less important. Especially the increase in the number of units with strong linkages with the local larger-scale sector has been impressive in the last years.
The bargaining strength of small-scale units with respect to the local larger-scale sector, the main client, is in general rather slight, and this is especially true for units in the sector that produces inputs for other industries (input sector). Mainly technician-entrepreneurs face difficulties in establishing the essential right contacts with the purchasing officers of the larger-scale units.

Survey data indicate that at least 20% of the units in town and 10% of those on the estates can be called 'sick'. The units in difficulties are mostly found in the input sector. In this sector in town, 25% make real losses, while another 50% is more or less keeping their business alive. At the same time, around 40% of the units in town and 70% of those on the estates are making good, or high, profits. This means that the units on the estates are far more profitable. In terms of generation of employment at a low cost of investment, the picture is reversed. Here the units in town create employment at a far lower level of investment. Since employment generation is an important goal of the government policy, this means that incentives should be geared more to small-scale units in town.

Small-scale units, especially in the input sector, face structural constraints. The more profitable types of subcontracting are mostly given to small-scale units in Bangalore and Madras. In Hosur, mainly the rougher subcontracting work is done. If the input sector would become more competitive with small-scale units in Bangalore, its position might improve. This would be possible only if the larger-scale sector used the local small-scale sector for more specialized phases of its production process, and if certain assurances were given. It is not likely that such a development will, in general, take place. There are nevertheless, a number of small-scale entrepreneurs who have succeeded in developing in just this way, because they have the right contacts and/or possess specialized knowledge.

On the small-scale estates, all units, in one way or another, supply the larger-scale sector. Producers of finished products on the estates supply them directly, or they market their products through wholesalers. The finished-product sector in town, the most traditional one, is the only sector that works for a substantial part (44%) for local needs. The input sector, both in town and on the small-scale estates, almost completely depends on orders from the, predominantly locally based, larger-scale sector.

Lack of working capital is a serious constraint on growth faced especially by very small units and technician-entrepreneurs, since they have less access to financial institutions. Here, the government can play a role, by providing working capital. Of course, this would be only a partial solution and a symptomatic approach.

Small-scale units producing finished products operate, in general, rather independently. Their prospects in a growing Hosur are in itself good. Small-scale units in the input sector are by nature dependent on larger-scale units for orders. Specialized small-scale units can obtain a reasonable independent position based on their bargaining strength. A 'true' ancillarization, with secured workload at reasonable prices and technical assistance, could solve the problems of irregularity in orders and lack of working capital. In the present circumstances, however, ancillarization is only to the benefit of the larger-scale sector. For small-scale units undertaking job-work the question is not whether ancillarization is desirable; but whether an ancillarization that is beneficial to them is feasible in today's India.

9.2 Population movements

The expansion of economic activities in the last ten years has lead to considerable changes in the demographic structure of Hosur. This is an important topic since one of the goals of the growth pole policy is involved. If the policy only benefits in-migrants from outside the region while the local population does not take part in the growth, one can hardly speak of regional development.

The migration rate is in Tamil Nadu slightly lower than in whole India: 35.2% versus 39.3% of the population has been born outside the place of

enumeration. The situation in Hosur is quite different from whole Tamil Nadu, as could be expected. Not only is the migration rate much higher, but also the distribution among the places of origin differs.
The migration from rural areas in the Dharmapuri district to Hosur is relative low. This does not mean that the surrounding rural areas supply less migrants than elsewhere in the state: if the intra-district rural migration is measured as percentage of the total population in the destination urban area, the differences are small (10.0% in Hosur versus 11.3% in Tamil Nadu).
The migration from urban areas elsewhere in the State and from urban areas in other states is exceptionally high. It is immediately clear that the fast growth of Hosur in recent years is caused by in-migration from other urban areas, mainly outside the district. The sexe division is also quite different from the Tamil Nadu situation. In the whole state the female outnumber the male in intra-district migration and participate slightly less in the other types of migration. In Hosur the intra-district migration from rural areas is equal among men and women, while the migration from urban areas elsewhere in the state is dominated by men. Remarkable is the higher migration of women from (urban areas in) other states compared to men.
The short distance migration within the district from rural areas is in Dharmapuri higher than in whole Tamil Nadu, as is the inter-district migration from urban areas. Hosur is different from Dharmapuri in that the 'short-rural' migration is much lower, and even less than in whole Tamil Nadu, while the inter-district migration from urban areas is higher than in Dharmapuri (that itself is already substantial compared to Tamil Nadu).
The majority of the migrants are young men, often bachelors. Indirect migration effects of the growth of Hosur have been minor: the migration from the rural hinterland has not increased substantially. Some of the workers from the district have found a job in the Sipcot industries, though only on the lower paid levels.

It has been found that commuting is not an important phenomenon in the mobility structure of Hosur. Less than 10% of the employees at the industrial areas comes daily from outside. The commuters form a rather heterogeneous group. The richer workers among them give hardly any contribution to the development of Hosur because of their preference to reside in the metropole Bangalore. The poorer commuters come in particular from the small towns and not from the villages where the majority of the population lives. At the moment this group has no plans to go to Hosur, thus the rural areas do have some (minor) benefits from the economic activities in Hosur. But most of the commuters are young, dependent members of households and it is not impossible that in the near future, after a change in marital status their opinions may change.

The income derived from commuting is necessary to cope with the expenses that have to be met daily, so almost nothing remains for other purposes. In many cases the economic future of the commuter households is highly insecure, because the job the commuter occupies is insecure, while his contribution to the household income is important, if not vital. Those households that for their income rely entirely on the commuters income could well be more vulnerable then ever. The data showed that the households that owned any properties were only slightly better off.

The rapid rise of population has completely changed the traditional social structure of Hosur. In-migration of young, skilled workers from Bangalore, Madras and other metropolitan areas has lead to disturbances in the demographic structure, making the age-structure unbalanced. The migration and the commuting from the surrounding countryside are insignificant. So we can conclude that the 'demographic' trickle-down effects of the growth pole policy to the backward Dharmapuri district are limited. The demographic future of Hosur is primarily in the hands of the group bachelors. If they start families this will lead to a sustainable population growth, but if they decide to leave the town, the industrial development will remain an enclave.

9.3 Labor and families

In his impressive study of factory labor in Bangalore (1976) Mark Holmström has used the image of the 'citadel' to describe the position of the 'protected' skilled workers in the modern sector of the economy. In later work (1984) he has strongly criticized this image. The organized/unorganized boundary is to his opinion not a wall but a steep slope. Indian society is like a mountain (see figure 9.1), with the very rich at the top, lush Alpine pastures where skilled workers in the biggest modern industries graze, a gradual slope down through smaller firms where pay and conditions are worse and the legal security of employment means less, a steep slope around the area where the Factories Act ceases to apply (the former wall of the citadel), a plateau where custom and the market give poorly paid unorganized sector workers some minimal security, then a long slope down through casual migrant labor and petty services to destitution. There are well-defined paths up and down these slopes, which are easiest for certain kinds of people.

Between the organized and unorganized sector there is a growing special market, where work - under cheap conditions of the informal sector - is done for the formal labor market. This shadow labor market deals with work outside the monetary sector. Ivan Illich (1982), who coined the term, uses 'shadow labor' to describe the historical development process of colonialism and capitalism. Since the introduction of the monetary system in every society, a variable part of total labor can be qualified as 'shadow labor'. Which part of communal labor precisely is unpaid depends upon political and economical decisions.
At the level of the individual household, economic wealth and the prevailing ideology play an important role. The division of unpaid work between the sexes however is pretty fixed: as long as women are part of the household, men will not do unpaid work in the household. Taking care of drinking water, laundry and

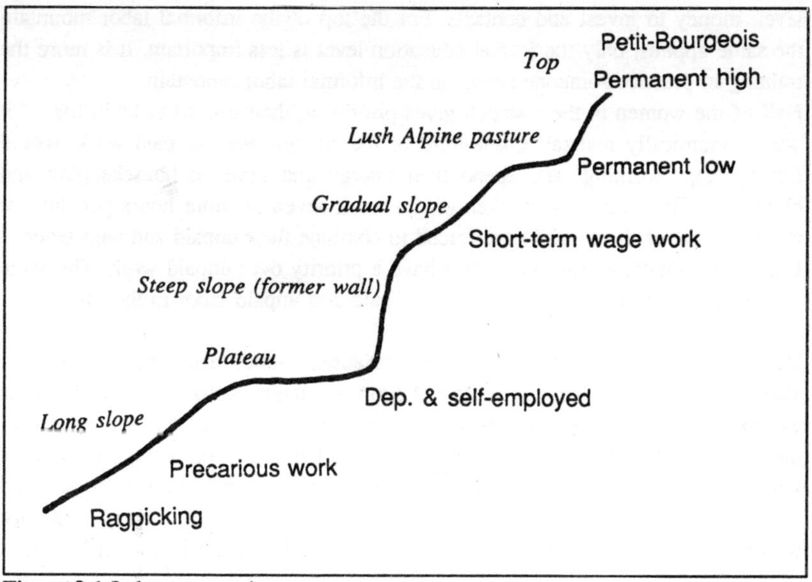

Figure 9.1 Labor mountain

food are in the first instance women's tasks. Men take on 'management tasks', like dealing with government agencies.

Besides the privileged skilled workers in the factories one can find a rising number of unskilled laborers. It concerns casual laborers who work in workshops or in the building industry or have to make a living from the collection of rags in the streets. The improvement of the labor-conditions of the permanent and registered short-term wage workers can be realized if labor-legislation will be improved and executed. The negotiation position of construction laborers is very weak. They have time nor knowledge to set up labor organizations.
Female labor has an overrepresentation in the lower paid, less attractive jobs of the labor market. The position of women is dependent of their family situation and stage in the life cycle. On the deforested hills of Hosur the ragpickers have to make a living. Mostly they lack patta; they are 'disenfranchised' (not registered on the voters list) and do not possess rationcards.

9.3.1 Mobility in a mountainous landscape

If we want to know which mobility exists between the segments, the labor market models are too static. Furthermore they do not show the combinations of labor categories women can make per day. The labor markets in Hosur look more like a mountainous landscape, with two tops (of the formal and informal labor markets) lying at a bottom of shadow labor. Mobility is frequent between the lower segments but the 'aristocracy' at the top of the formal and informal mountains are not willing to let in strangers (Harriss, 1986). One only comes in the area of permanent wage labor if he or she has disposal of a good educational

level, money to invest and contacts. For the top of the informal labor mountain the same applies; only the formal education level is less important. It is more the training in practice someone needs on the informal labor mountain.
Half of the women in the research gives priority to their unpaid tasks in life. If it was economically realizable, one-third of the women who do paid work, would like to stop 'working' and spend their energy and time on housekeeping and child care. However most women (86%) work seven or more hours per day for money. Most of them (63%) are forced to combine their unpaid and paid labor. For nearly one-third paid work does have a priority over unpaid work. The same part is pleased to make a combination of paid and unpaid labor in their lives.

Best help to get a better job is recommendation. Money and time to invest are also important resources as is the support of their husband or father. It is extremely difficult for women to act in public without the permission of dominant male family members. Education is of minor importance. The women who want to get more education, prefer general education in basics: to read and write, bookkeeping and industrial training for work in a factory. Schools, however, with informal education for unskilled adults are not known in Hosur.

Growth pole policy could create employment for women, provided that applied education is accessible for women and there are facilities of favorable credit allowance for women only. If credit facilities are sexe-neutral, men push female lenders away. Female home-based and casual workers get better employment when the work of middleman and labor broker are taken over by themselves. In that case they have control over their own labor and the earnings.
Female employees at the hills and top of the formal labor mountain migrated from urban environments. They have applied for one of the available women's jobs at the formal labor market. Given the fact that there are only a few female labor factories in and around Hosur (electronics and fruit canning) the market is filled quickly.
Contrary to the aims of growth pole policy, especially rural migrants and local women have no benefits of this policy. In Hosur they are forced to take the marginal work, left over by men, e.g. watercarriers. Compared with the position of women in peasant communities their life becomes more uncertain, and their position even more marginal. In this way the current growth pole policy cannot be called an improvement for women's life.

9.3.2 Ragpickers

Apart from the better off people, also poor people from the surrounding areas come to Hosur in search for jobs. Due to their low level of education (if any) there are not many jobs in the industrial area for them. They have to make their living in the traditional informal economy. Some are successful, but a growing portion of them are not. Amongst the latter group are the people that earn their living with 'ragpicking'. Ragpicking is a hard way to make a living. It is dirty, heavy and unhealthy work which puts a great strain on the physical condition of the ragpickers. It is likely, considering their number, that ragpickers contribute in a large extent to the cleaning of the streets and the recycling of waste materials. The fact that more than 60% of this group is below the age of 16 is pointing to the fact that many children have to take up ragpicking early to contribute to the householdincome. The illiteracy rate amongst the ragpickers is nearly total and there is no additional money for schooling available. Almost half of the approached families is in debt and the income generated from ragpicking forms for the greater part the householdincome, which marks the low income of the ragpickers. Within the broken families women and children have to earn the little amount of money. Some ragpickers do not have any shelter at all and sleep on the streets or under the rocks. Almost all of them migrated to Hosur.

The ragpickers are socially isolated which manifests itself in the absence of contacts with people in Hosur other than relatives or people from the same 'caste'; they go to special kinds of hotels, teashops etcetera. The Harijans in this particular case are even 'more untouchable' due to the kind of work they are doing which in the Hindu society is regarded as very inferior. A consequence of this isolation is their difficulty (or absence) to have contacts with governmental institutions (their illiteracy also plays a role). All facilities for which it is needed to approach the government (for instance ration cards, patta, registration on the voting list) are not available for ragpickers. The costs of living in Hosur are rising rapidly while the income of the poorest is more stable leading to a further deterioration of this group. Birkbeck (1980) considers ragpicking as a refugee-job but in Hosur it became clear that ragpicking is an activity needed to survive.

Ragpickers are ignored by the local government and can be regarded as the drawback of the growth pole policy. Only the more well-to-do people, who are employed in the industries, benefited from the government policy. In this way the government policy did increase the inequalities within Hosur.

9.4 Relations of power

In the discussion on survival and livelihood family and household play an important role as the smallest units of analysis. Households are characterized by relations of power which are heavily influenced by the access of adult householdmembers to the outside world, such as having a job or running a small business. The job or business can be turned into a power base in the struggle for household domination. This becomes especially apparent when women, whose usual occupation is at home, begin to enter the labor market, earning a little money of their own. Financial independence is not usually appreciated by the male member of the family, though it increasingly is the only way that households can meet critical needs. Broken families are sometimes the result.
Poor families are severely limited in the kinds of choices they can make. Domestic activities consume an enormous amount of time: eighty to ninety hours

of women's work a week is not unusual. This includes paid labor and unpaid labor as well. The unpaid labor of women consists of the care for the household.

One of the household tasks is the supply of water. In the better off residential areas private tap connections are available. This does not mean that water is running all day. Only a part of the day water is available. So a person has to wait for the water to come. In the poorer residential areas with no private tap connection, women are dependent of public sources. This is a more time consuming and tiring activity than to wait for the water from the tap. Not all the public sources give reliable drinking water. In former times all the sources had water of good quality. After the establishment of the big industries the quality has fallen. The water requirements for the industries and the irrigated agriculture are subtracted from the ground water. As a consequence the water-table has fallen, so the original sources became salty. It will be clear that the poorer groups in Hosur are affected mostly by the decrease of the water quality. Investments have been made for the water supply of the commercial sector and hardly for the local population.

An iron minimum of cash is needed to buy essential food, transportation and clothing. So the necessary time must be saved from other activities to ensure that a minimum cash flows into the domestic economy. But the needs of most households are likely to exceed this minimum.

Being poor is usually defined by those who are not poor, such as bureaucrats or social workers, in terms of low income. In the extreme case of 'absolute' poverty, a more physical measure may be used, such as caloric intake (Gulatti 1981). Those who fall below an imaginary 'poverty line' are defined as poor. It would be more accurate, however, to speak of poverty as condition of relative powerlessness. Power in this case does not mean economic power, but in the first place social and political power.

The poor no longer appear as 'consumers' (low-income persons) but as producers of their livelihood. There is very little that the powerless household can do to improve its own situation, unless it joins with other households in organization and struggle. It is for this reason that we can speak of the process as one of *collective self-empowerment.* However this way of speaking seems to suggest that the poor can escape poverty simply by joining in community-based efforts. This is an oversimplification: cooperation and organization are necessary but not sufficient conditions. What is needed as well is a state whose social policies facilitate, complement and support community efforts and self-empowerment. For instance, only the state (local government) can legalize access to urban land by distributing patta.

Experience of the poorest people in their relation with the state has been largely one of antagonistic struggle. Confrontations with police and politicians are part of almost everyone's history, which is etched deeply in their memories. Some have a more bitter story to tell, recalling how families were uprooted and displaced towards a more distant periphery of the town.

What poor people need above everything is greater social and political power. The state cannot solve the problem of disenfranchisement and massive poverty. More important is the question whether the state is prepared to support the process of collective self-empowerment of the poorest families.

The growth pole policy did make of Hosur an island with prosperous factories in a backward district, but left a growing group of vulnerable families with few opportunities.

LITERATURE

ACKERMANS, A. and J. BETH 1987
Ongeschoolde bouwarbeiders/sters in Hosur. Amsterdam.
AMSDEN, A.H. (ed.) 1980
The economics of women and work. Penguin Books. Middlesex, England.
ANKER, R. 1983
Female labour force participation in developing countries. A critique of current definitions and data collection methods. In: International Labour Review, Vol. 122, No. 6, pp. 709-723.
AZIZ, A. 1984
Urban poor and urban informal sector. Institute for Social and Economic Change. Bangalore.
BANERJEE, N. 1985
Women workers in the unorganized sector: the Calcutta experience. Sangam Books. Hyderabad.
BANERJEE, N. and D. JAIN (eds.) 1985
Women in poverty: tyranny of the household. Investigative Essays on Women's Work. Shaktibooks, Vikas Publishing House. New Delhi.
BASTER, N. 1981
The measurement of women's participation in development: the use of census data. Sussex.
BAUD, I.S.A. 1983
Women's labor in the Indian textile industry: the influence of technology and organization on the gender division of labor. IVO-Katholieke Universiteit Brabant.
BAUD, I.S.A. 1991
Forms of production an women's labor: Gender aspects of industrialization in India and Mexico. Sage. New Dehli.
BENERIA, L. and M. ROLDAN 1987
The crossroads of class and gender. Industrial homework, subcontracting and household dynamics in Mexico City. University of Chicago Press. Chicago.
BERGMANN, B.R. 1980
Occupational segregation, wages and profits when employers discriminate by race or sex. In: A. Amsden. The economics of women and work.
BHARATHAN, K. 1981
Development through industrialization: an analysis and case-study of backward area development (Hosur, Tamil Nadu). Madras Institute of Development Studies, Working Paper No. 24. Madras.
BHATTY, Z. 1984
Economic role and status of women: a case-study of women in the beedi-industry in Allahabad. WEP 15, ILO. Geneva.
BILSBORROW, R.E., A.S. OBERAI and G. STANDING 1984
Migration surveys in low-income countries, ILO, Croom Helm. Kent.

BIRKBECK, C.H. 1979
Garbage, industry and the 'vultures' of Cali, Colombia. In: Bromley and Gerry (eds), pp. 161-184. London.

BLAKE, M. (not dated)
Case studies on women in the informal sector.

BLINCOW, M. 1986
Scavengers and recycling: a neglected domain of production. In: Labour, Capital and Society, Vol. 19, No. 1.

BREMAN, J.C. 1976
A dualistic labour system? A critique of the 'informal sector' concept. In: Economic and Political Weekly, Vol. 11, No. 48, pp. 1870-1876, No. 49, pp. 1905-1908, No. 50, pp. 1939-1944.

BROMLEY, R. (ed.) 1985
Planning for small enterprises in Third World cities. Exeter.

BROMLEY, R. 1988
Working in the streets: survival strategy, necessity or unavoidable evil? In: J. Gugler (ed.). The urbanisation of the third world. Pp. 161-181.

BROMLEY, R. and C. BIRKBECK 1988
Urban economy and employment. In: M. Pacione: Geography of the third world, p. 114-147. London.

BROMLEY, R. and C. GERRY 1979
Casual work and poverty in the third world cities. Chicester.

BRUIJNE, G.A. de, P. ROBBEN and J.J.F. HEINS 1983
Agropolitan development, small scale activities and building in Tamil Nadu: some theoretical reflexions. The Indian Geographical Journal, Vol. 58, No. 1. Madras.

CARLSTEIN, T. 1982
Time resources, society and ecology. Vol 1. Pre-industrial Societies. Allen and Unwin Ltd. London.

CENSUS OF INDIA 1971 1978
Migration tables, Series 19, Tamil Nadu, Part II-D. Madras.

CENSUS OF INDIA 1981 1983
Series 20, Tamil Nadu, Part II-A. Madras.

CHAMBERS, R. 1985
The Working Women's Forum: A counter culture by poor women. Unicef Regional Office for South Central Asia; Women's Development Section. New Delhi.

EEKHOUT, J. 1987
Azen op afval: de vuilnisrapers onder oude en nieuwe vormen van kapitalisme. Doctoraalscriptie Culturele Antropologie, Rijks Universiteit Utrecht.

EL-HAKIM, S.M. 1977
The role of the family, kinship and rural/urban migration in processing of solid waste in Cairo. In: Africa Development, Vol. 2, No.2, pp. 115-122.

FERREE, M. M. and J.G. GUGLER 1984
The participation of women in the urban labor force and in rural-urban migration in India. Working Paper 46. Connecticut.

FRIEDMANN, J. 1991
Empowerment. The politics of alternative development. Basil Blackwell. Oxford.
FRIEDMANN, J. and C. WEAVER 1979
Territory and function. Edward Arnold. London.
FUREDY, C. 1984
From urban fringe and elite suburb: scavening and recuperation by the urban poor in Calcutta. In: Geojournal, Vol. 8, No. 2.
FUREDY, C 1989
Social considerations in solid waste management in Asian cities. In: Regional Development Dialogue. Vol. 10, No. 3, pp. 13-43.
GARELLA, V. 1985
Marginal informal activities in a metropolis: a study of waste collectors ITO-area, New Dehli. In: SPA Journal of School of Planning and Architecture, pp. 159-167. New Dehli.
GUGLER, J. (ed.) 1988
The urbanization of the third world. Oxford University Press. Oxford.
GULATI, L. 1981
Profiles in female poverty: a study of five poor working women in Kerala. Hindustan Publishing Corporation India. New Delhi.
HACKENBERG, B. and G. BARTH 1984
Growth of the bazaar economy and its significance for women's employment: trends of the 1970's in Davao, Philippines. In: G.W. Jones, Women in the urban and industrial work force, pp. 259-277.
HÄGERSTRAND, T. 1978
Survivals and arena. On the life-history of individuals in relation to their geographical environment. In: Human Activity and Time Geography, Vol. 2, pp. 122-145, T. Carlstein, D. Parker and N. Thrift (eds). Edward Arnold. London.
HARDOY, J.E. and D. SATTERTHWAITE (eds) 1986
Small and intermediate urban centers. Their role in national and regional development in the third world. Hodder and Stoughton. London.
HARRISS, B. 1987
Regional growth linkages from agriculture and resource flows in non-farm economy. In: Economic and Political Weekly, June 5, pp. 945-953, June 12, pp. 973-1001.
HARRISS, J. 1982
Character of an urban economy: small-scale production and labor markets in Coimbatore. In: Economic and Political Weekly, June 5 and 12.
HARRISS, J. 1985
Our socialism and the subsistence engineer. In: R. Bromley, Planning for small enterprises in third world cities.
HARRISS, J. 1986
Vulnerable workers in the labor markets of South and South-East Asia. Norwich.
HARRISS, J. 1986
The working poor and the labor aristocracy in a South Indian city: a descriptive and analytical account. In: Modern Asian Studies, Vol. 20, pp. 231-285.

HARRISS, J., K.P. KANNAN and G. RODGERS (1990)
Urban labor market structure and job access in India: A study of Coimbatore. Research series No. 92. International Institute for Labor Studies. Geneva. Center for Development Studies. Trivandrum.

HEYINK LEESTEMAKER, J., M. NOLTEN and I. TOM (eds) 1989
Geography in development; Feminist perspectives on development geography. ASGS, No. 24. University of Amsterdam.

HEYZER, N. 1981
Women, subsistence and the informal sector: towards a framework of analysis. Discussion Paper IDS. Sussex.

HEYZER, N. 1985
From rural subsistence to an industrial peripheral work force: an examination of female Malaysian migrants and capital accumulation in Singapore. In: L. Beneria (ed.), Women and Development. Sexual division of labor in rural societies, pp. 179-203. Praeger. New York.

HEYZER, N. 1986
Working women in South-East Asia: development, subordination and emancipation. Alden Press. Oxford.

HOLMSTRÖM, M. 1976
South-Indian factory workers: their live and their work. Cambridge University Press. London.

HOLMSTRÖM, M. 1984
Industry and inequality: the social anthropology of indian labor. Cambridge.

HUIJSTEE, W.P. van, 1987
Commuting to Hosur. The spatial mobility of labor in a peripheral district of Tamil Nadu, India. M.A.-thesis. Amsterdam.

ILLICH, I. 1982
Gender. Marion Boyars Publishers Ltd. London.

JAIN, D. 1980
Street vendors of Ahmedabad. In: Women's quest for power. Five case-studies. Sahibabad Distt., Vikas Publishing House PVT Ltd. Ghaziabad, U.P., India.

JAIN, D., N. SING and M. CHAND 1979
Women's work: methodological issues. In: Women and development, Perspectives from South and South East Asia. R. Jahan and H. Papanek (eds), pp. 152-170.

JONES, G.W. (ed) 1984
Women in the urban and industrial work force. Southeast and East Asia. DSC Monograph (33), Australian National University. Hawaii Press. Honolulu, USA.

KALPAGAM, U. 1983
Women and urban poverty-issues from case-studies of three families. In: Popular series Nr. 5., pp. 1-43. Madras Institute of Development Studies.

KALPAGAM, U. 1984
Labor market segmentation in a multi-structural context: implications for India's female labor force. In: Labor, Capital and Society 17:2 November, pp. 196-221.

KALPAGAM, U. 1985
Coping with urban poverty in India. In: Bulletin of Concerned Asian Scholars, Vol. 17, pp. 2-18.
KNORRINGA, P. 1989
The small-scale sector in a growth pole. A case study of Hosur, Tamil Nadu, India. No. 7, CASA. Amsterdam.
KERKUM, N.M. 1990
Een tip van de sluier. Een onderzoek naar het dagelijks leven van vuilrapers in Hosur, Zuid-India. Doktoraal skriptie sociale geografie. Universiteit van Amsterdam.
LIDDLE, J. and R. JOSHI 1986
Daughters of independence. Gender, caste and class in India. Zen Books Ltd. London.
LOOP van der, T.H.M. 1984
De structuur van de (woning)bouwsector in Mali en Senegal. De produktiewijze-theorie toegepast. Geografische en Planologische notitie. Vrije universiteit. Amsterdam.
LOOP van der, T.H.M. 1988
The structure of the building sector in a medium-sized city: Contractors, jobbers and hutmakers in Vellore (Tamil Nadu, India). No. 7, CASA. Amsterdam.
MADRAS INSTITUTE OF DEVELOPMENT STUDIES 1988
Tamil Nadu economy: performance and issues. Madras.
MEIJER, E.N. and J.J.F. HEINS 1985
Migration to a growth pole in a backward district of Tamil Nadu, India. The Indian Geographical Journal, Vol. 60, No. 2.
MEIJER, E.N. and J.J.F. HEINS 1987
Growth pole policy and population movements; migration and commuting to Hosur. Seminar paper. Utrecht. Discussie stukken vakgroep geografie van de ontwikkelingslanden, No. 36. Amsterdam.
MIES, M. 1983
Indian Women in subsistence and agricultural labor. Assisted by K. Lalitha and Krishna Kumari. WEP 10/WP 34, ILO. Geneva.
MIES, M. 1985
The dynamics of the sexual division of labor and integration of rural women into the world market. In: L. Beneria (ed.). Women and Development, pp. 1-29.
MOAVENZADEH, F. 1978
Construction industry in developing countries. In: World Development, Vol. 6, pp. 97-116.
MOHAN, R. 1983
India: coming to terms with urbanization. In: Cities, Vol. 1, pp. 46-58.
MUKERJEE, S. 1975
Under the shadow of the metropolis. They are citizens too. Calcutta.
NAGARAJ, R. 1984
Subcontracting in Indian manufacturing industries: analysis, evidence and issues. In: Economic and Political Weekly, August, pp. 135-1453.

NAIR, A. and F. WILLEKENS 1982
The data base for migration analysis in developing countries: with an emphasis on India, NIDI Working Paper, No. 28, Voorburg.

OBERAI, A.S. 1983
An overview of migration influencing policies and programmes. In: A.S. Oberai (ed.). State policies and internal migration. Studies in market and planned economies. ILO, Croom Helm Ltd, London and Canberra.

PANINI, M.N. 1978
Networks and styles: A study of Faridabad industrial entrepreneurs. In: Process and institution in urban India, sociological studies. S. Saberwal (ed.). Vikas Publishing House. New Dehli.

PANSTERS, W.G. 1985
Petty commodity production and social relations of production: the case of Ciudad Juarez, Mexico. In: Bolletin de Estudios Latinoamericanos y del Caribe, No. 39, pp. 45-63.

PRABHAKARA, N.R. 1986
Internal migration and population redistribution in India. Concept Publishing Company. New Delhi.

PREMI, M.K. and J.A.L. TOM 1985
City characteristics, migration, and urban development policies in India. Papers of the East-West Population Institute, No. 92. Honolulu.

RAMANCHANDRAN 1980
The role of science and technology in improving human settlements. In: Habitat International.

RAMASWAMY, E.A. and U. RAMASWAMY 1981
Industry and labor, an introduction. New Delhi.

REDCLIFT, N. 1985
The contested domain: gender, accumulation and the labor process. In: Beyond Employment, pp. 92-127. Basil Blackwell Ltd. Oxford.

REICH, M., D.M. GORDON and R.C. EDWARDS 1980
A theory of labor market segmentation. In: A. Amsden. The economics of women and work, pp. 232-242.

ROELOFS, A. and T.H.M. van der LOOP 1985
Gestructureerde informaliteit: De bouwsector in Vellore (India) en de rol van de vrouwelijke bouwvakkers. Bijdrage in het kader van het internationale jaar van de daklozen. Amsterdam.

ROSSI, A.S. 1981
Life-span theories and women's lives. In: Signs, Vol. 6 (1), pp. 4-32. University of Chicago.

SALEM GAZETEER 1918

SCHENK-SANDBERGEN, L. 1982
Women's work without status. Outdoor household - servants in Allepey (Kerala, India). Working Paper Nr. 18. Amsterdam.

SCOTT, J.W. and I.A. TILLY 1980
Women's work and the family in nineteenth-century Europe. In: A. Amsden. The economics of women and work. pp. 91-125.

SELIER, F. and M.S. KARIM (eds) 1986
Migration in Pakistan; facts and theories. Vanguard Books. Lahore.

SIPCOT 1984
Guide to entrepreneurs. Government of Tamil Nadu. Madras.
STANDING, G. 1982
Conceptualising territorial mobility in low-income countries. ILO. Geneva.
STATE PLANNING COMMISSION 1974
The perspective plan for Tamil Nadu 1974-84. Madras.
STATISTICAL ATLAS 1908
Salem District.
STRETTON, A. 1979
Instability of employment among building industry laborers in Manilla. In: Bromley and Gerry. Casual work and poverty in third world cities.
TERMOTE, M. 1975
The measurement of commuting. In: S. Goldstein and D.F. Sly. The measurement of urbanization and projection of urban population, pp. 211-224. Liege.
TYABIJI, N. 1984
Nature of small enterprise development: political aims and socio-economic reality. In: Economic and Political Weekly, August, pp. 1425-1433.
WONG, S.T. and KHALID M.S. 1984
Comparison of the economic impacts of six growth centers on their surrounding rural areas in Asia In: H.D. Kammeier and P.J. Swan (eds). Equity with growth? Planning perspectives for small towns in developing countries. Asian Institute of Technology. Bangkok.